ArcGIS® 9

Linear Referencing in ArcGIS

DATA CREDITS

Highways and streets map—Maryland Department of Transportation State Highway Administration, Baltimore, Maryland

Transit map—Parsons Brinckerhoff Quade & Douglas, Inc., Los Angeles, California

Railways map—Parsons Brinckerhoff Quade & Douglas, Inc., Los Angeles, California

Oil and gas exploration map—TGS–NOPEC Geophysical Company, Houston, Texas

Pipelines map—M.J. Harden Associates, Inc., Kansas City, Missouri

Water resources map—Center for Research in Water Resources, University of Texas at Austin

Hatching map 1—New York State Department of Transportation, Albany, New York

Hatching map 2—TGS–NOPEC Geophysical Company, Houston, Texas

AUTHORS

Patrick Brennan, Melanie Harlow

Contents

Introduction

Many organizations collect data about linear *features*, such as highways, city streets, railroads, rivers, and pipelines as well as water and sewer networks. In most geographic information systems (GIS), these features are modeled in two dimensions, using x,y coordinates. While these systems work well for maintaining features with static characteristics, these organizations have realized that their linear features often have characteristics that are more dynamic in nature. To handle this, these organizations have developed one-dimensional linear referencing systems to model their data.

How these organizations store and utilize their linear referencing data varies not only between the organizations themselves but also between the departments within the organizations. Because of this variance, there is a need for flexible tools to create, display, query, analyze, and distribute linear referencing data.

ESRI® ArcGIS® software contains a series of easy-to-use tools, wizards, and dialog boxes that assist you in meeting your linear referencing needs. In this book, you will learn how to create, calibrate, edit, display, and query the data used in linear referencing.

Who uses linear referencing?

Most applications that use linear features can benefit from linear referencing. The following pages outline a few examples.

Highways and streets

Agencies that manage highways and streets use linear referencing in a variety of ways in their day-to-day operations. For example, linear referencing is useful for assessing pavement conditions; maintaining, managing, and valuing assets (e.g., traffic signs and signals, guard rails, toll booths, and loop detectors); organizing bridge management information; and reviewing and coordinating construction projects. Linear referencing also helps facilitate the creation of a common database that traffic planners, traffic engineers, and public works analysts can use for cross-disciplinary decision support.

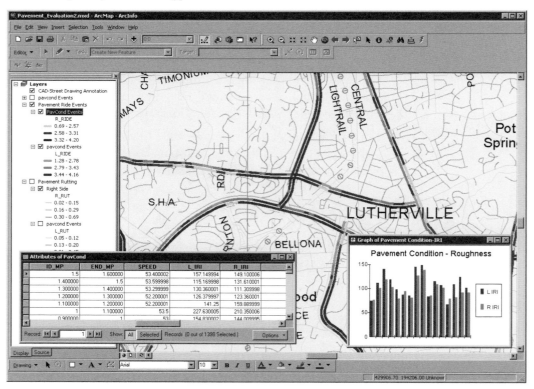

Pavement conditions along the highways that serve Baltimore, Maryland

LINEAR REFERENCING IN ARCGIS

Transit

Linear referencing is a key component in transit applications and facilitates such things as route planning and analysis; automatic vehicle location and tracking; bus stop and facility inventory; rail system facility management; track, power, communications, and signal maintenance; accident reporting and analysis; demographic analysis and route restructuring; ridership analysis and reporting; and transportation planning and modeling.

Corridor study showing the number of traffic accidents along an 18-mile stretch of the I-710 Freeway in Los Angeles County

Railways

Railways use linear referencing to manage key information for rail operations, maintenance, asset management, and decision support systems. Linear referencing makes it possible, for example, to select a line and track and identify milepost locations for bridges and other obstructions that would prevent various types of freight movement along the route. Further, dynamic segmentation can be used to display track characteristics as well as to view digital images of bridges and obstructions.

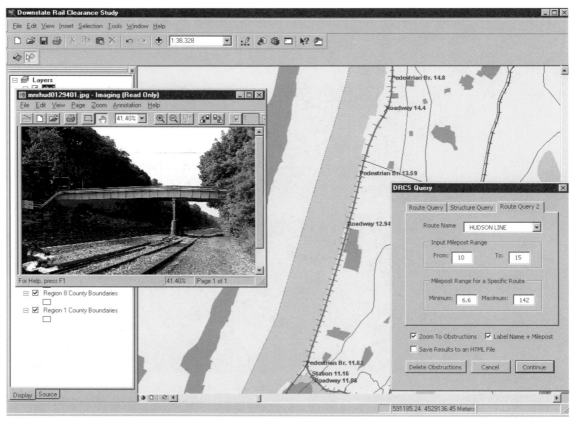

Analyzing rail clearances along the Hudson rail line in downstate New York

Oil and gas exploration

The petroleum industry manages tremendous volumes of data used in geophysical exploration. Seismic surveys, or shotpoint data, are used to help understand the underlying geology in an area. The nature of seismic data is that it must be represented as both a linear object—the seismic line—and a collection of point objects—the shotpoint. Both the seismic line and the individual shotpoints have *attributes*, both must be maintained at the same time, and both are used in modeling applications. Linear referencing helps solve this problem.

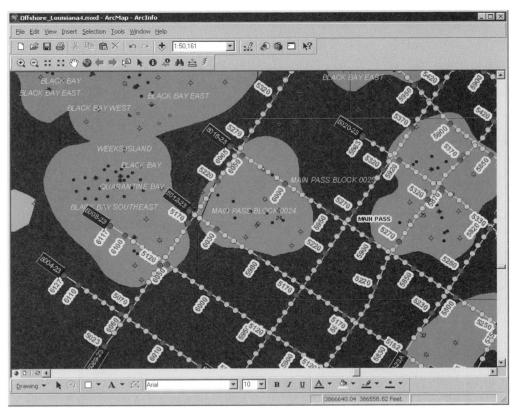

Posting and labeling seismic lines and shotpoints in the Gulf of Mexico off the Louisiana coast

Pipelines

In the pipeline industry, linear referencing is often referred to as stationing. *Stationing* allows any point along a pipeline to be uniquely identified. As such, stationing is useful for collecting and storing information regarding pipeline facilities; both inline and physical inspection histories; regulatory compliance information; risk assessment studies; work history events; and geographic information, such as environmentally sensitive areas, political boundaries (e.g., state and county), right-of-way boundaries, and various types of crossings.

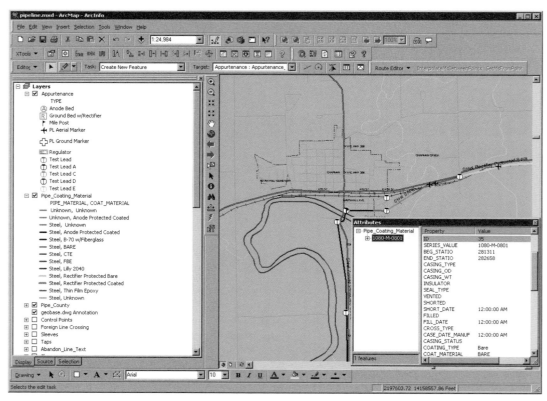

Pipeline coating material types in rural Kansas

Water resources

In hydrology applications, linear referencing is often called river addressing. *River addressing* allows objects, such as field monitoring stations, which collect information about water quality analysis, toxic release inventories, drinking water supplies, flow, and so on, to be located along a river or stream system. Further, the measurement scheme used in river addressing allows for the measurement of flow distance between any two points on a flow path.

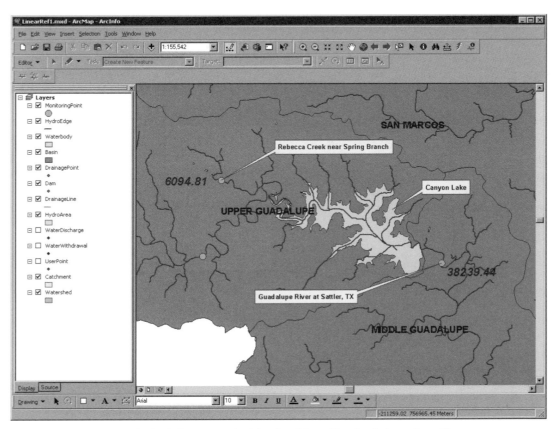

Monitoring stations along the hydrology network of the Guadalupe River basin in southern Texas

Tips on learning about linear referencing

If you're new to GIS, take some time to familiarize yourself with ArcGIS. The books *Using ArcCatalog*, *Using ArcMap*, *Editing in ArcMap*, *Building a Geodatabase*, and *Geoprocessing in ArcGIS* contain tutorials to show you how to create, edit, manage, and display GIS data.

Begin learning about linear referencing and dynamic segmentation in Chapter 2, 'Quick-start tutorial', in this book. In Chapter 2, you will learn how to create and calibrate route data, display and query route and event data, and edit route data. ArcGIS comes with the data used in this tutorial, so you can follow along step by step at your computer. You can also read the tutorial without using your computer.

Finding answers to your questions

Like most people, your goal is to complete your tasks while investing a minimum amount of time and effort in learning how to use software. You want intuitive, easy-to-use software that gives you immediate results without having to read pages of documentation. When you do have a question, however, you want the answer quickly so you can complete your task. That's what this book is all about—getting you the answers you need when you need them.

This book describes how to accomplish linear referencing tasks. Although you can read this book from start to finish, you'll likely use it more as a reference. When you want to know how to do a particular task, such as identifying a route location, just look it up in the table of contents or index. What you'll find is a concise, step-by-step description of how to complete the task. Some chapters also include detailed information that you can read if you want to learn more about the concepts behind the tasks. You may also refer to the glossary in this book if you come across any unfamiliar GIS terms or need to refresh your memory.

Getting help on your computer

In addition to this book, the ArcGIS Desktop Help system is a valuable resource for learning the software. To learn how to use Help, see *Using ArcMap*.

Contacting ESRI

If you need to contact ESRI for technical support, refer to 'Contacting Technical Support' in the 'Getting more help' section of the ArcGIS Desktop Help system. You can also visit ESRI on the Web at *www.esri.com* and *support.esri.com* for more information on linear referencing and ArcGIS.

ESRI education solutions

ESRI provides educational opportunities related to geographic information science, GIS applications, and technology. You can choose among instructor-led courses, Web-based courses, and self-study workbooks to find educational solutions that fit your learning style. For more information, go to *www.esri.com/ education*.

Quick-start tutorial

2

ArcGIS has the tools you need for linear referencing applications. The easiest way to start learning about linear referencing is to complete the exercises in this tutorial. Before you start, however, it is assumed you know the fundamentals of ArcGIS software. For more information, see *Geoprocessing in ArcGIS*, *Using ArcCatalog*, *Using ArcMap*, and *Editing in ArcMap*.

For this tutorial, imagine that you work in the GIS department of a highway authority responsible for the maintenance and safety of your region's highways. In the exercises to follow, you will perform some of the linear referencing tasks typical to such a person. Specifically, you will use the linear referencing tools in ArcToolbox™ to create and recalibrate route data. Next, you will learn how to display and query your newly created route data in ArcMap™. After that, you will discover how easy it is to display and query your route event data in ArcMap. Lastly, you will learn how to edit your route data in ArcMap.

The licenses required to complete each exercise vary from ArcView® to ArcEditor™ to ArcInfo™. If you require a license different from ArcView, it will be indicated at the top of the page. Even if you don't have the appropriate license, feel free to read through the exercises to familiarize yourself with the linear referencing functionality in ArcGIS.

This tutorial includes five exercises, each of which takes five to 30 minutes to complete. The exercises build on one another, so it is assumed that you will complete them in order.

The study area for this tutorial is Pitt County, North Carolina. The data was compiled from various sources and has been modified to suit the needs of the exercises. The reliability and suitability of the information, therefore, cannot be guaranteed.

Exercise 1: Organizing your data in ArcCatalog

The exercises in this chapter use the tutorial data distributed with ArcGIS and work with an ArcView license. Some of these exercises require you to make changes to the data, therefore, you will need to have write access to the data. To be sure you have write access, you will begin this exercise by making a working copy of the LinearReferencing tutorial folder.

Copying the data

1. Start ArcCatalog™ by either double-clicking a shortcut installed on your desktop or using the Programs list in your Start menu.

2. Navigate to the LinearReferencing folder on the local drive where the tutorial data is installed, for example, C:\arcgis\ArcTutor\LinearReferencing.

   If the data was installed by your system administrator in a shared folder on the network, the path to the tutorial folder includes the names of the computer and the connection through which the folder is accessed, for example,
   \\dataserver\public\ArcGIS\ArcTutor\LinearReferencing.

3. Right-click the Linear Referencing folder and click Copy.

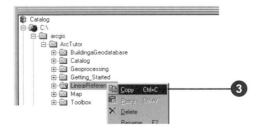

4. Navigate to the location where you would like to make a copy of this data, such as C:\.

5. Right-click this location and click Paste.

A new folder called Linear Referencing will be created at this location.

6. Right-click this new folder and click Rename. Enter "MyLR" as the new folder name.

Connect directly to your tutorial data

In ArcCatalog, folder connections let you access specific directories on local disks or shared folders on the network. Further, database connections allow you to access the contents of a database.

1. Click the Connect To Folder button on the Standard toolbar.

2. Navigate to and select your location of MyLR.

3. Click OK.

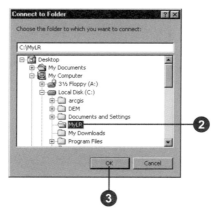

The new folder connection is now listed in the Catalog tree. You will now be able to access all of the data needed for the remaining exercises in this tutorial via the new connection.

Exercise 2: Creating and calibrating route data

The first thing you will need for any linear referencing project is accurate route data. In this exercise, you use ArcToolbox tools to create and calibrate route data. The first activity is to create a temporary layer representing only the line features that have route and measure information stored as attribute values. Next, you will create a route feature class by merging the input line features of the temporary layer that share a common route identifier. Finally, you will recalibrate the newly created routes using a point feature class storing route and measure information as attributes.

Creating a layer

Not every feature in the base_roads feature class has route and measure information. Therefore, before any routes are created, you will want to isolate only those routes that contain this information. Creating routes using features that do not have this information would be pointless.

Creating a temporary layer allows you to do things, such as make selections, without affecting the original data source. This layer will not appear in the ArcCatalog contents, because it is created in-memory and simply references the data stored on disk. These layers can be used as inputs to other geoprocessing tools within your working session. Once you exit the application the in-memory layers will be removed.

1. In ArcCatalog, show the ArcToolbox window by clicking the Show/Hide ArcToolbox button on the Standard toolbar.

You can click the top of the ArcToobox window and drag it around the ArcCatalog window to dock it where you prefer. Also try double-clicking the top of the window to undock or dock it.

2. Expand the Data Management Tools toolbox to show its contents.

3. Expand the Layers and Table Views toolset to show its contents.

4. Right-click the Make Feature Layer tool and click Open. Alternatively you can double-click the Make Feature Layer tool to open it.

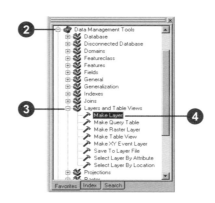

There are several ways to set the input feature class. You can drag a feature class from the ArcCatalog tree and drop it onto the text box, click the Browse button and navigate to the feature class in the dialog box, or simply type the full pathname to the feature class in the text box.

The tutorial instructions will simply ask you to type names and paths into the appropriate text boxes. Feel free, however, to use any of the available techniques.

5. Type "C:\MyLR\PITT.mdb\PITT\base_roads" for the value of the Input Features parameter.

6. Type "measured_roads" for the value of the Layer Name parameter.

7. Click the Expression button to open the Query Builder dialog box.

8. Type "[ROUTE1] <> 0" in the text box.

9. Click OK on the Query Builder dialog box.

10. Click OK on the Make Layer dialog box.

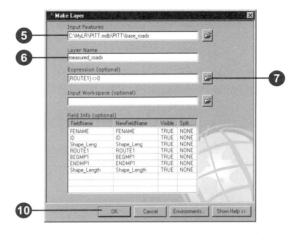

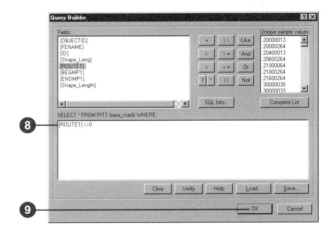

The tool's progress dialog box opens as the tool runs.

11. Click Close on the tool's progress dialog box when the process is finished.

ArcInfo and ArcEditor

Creating route data

The Create Routes tool is used to specify the input line features, the route identifier field, the method used to set the route measures, and the output feature class. Note that the input features can be any supported format. This includes coverage, shapefile, personal and enterprise geodatabase, and *computer-aided design (CAD)* data.

1. Expand the Linear Referencing Tools toolset to show its contents.

2. Right-click the Create Routes tool and click Open.

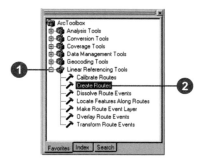

3. Click the dropdown arrow for the Input Line Features and click the measured_roads layer.

4. Click the Route Identifier Field dropdown arrow and click ROUTE1. The values in the route identifier field uniquely identify each route.

Next, you need to specify the name for the output feature class. This feature class can be contained within the same geodatabase as the input, or you can save it to another geodatabase or shapefile. If it is saved to a geodatabase it can be contained within a feature dataset or on its own as a feature class. For this exercise you will be writing the new data to the same feature dataset as the input.

5. Type "C:\MyLR\PITT.mdb\PITT\routes" for the value of the Output Route Feature Class parameter.

Next specify how the route measures will be obtained. There are three choices:

- Geometric lengths of the input features are used to accumulate the measures.

- Values stored in a measure field are used to accumulate the measures.

- Values stored in from- and to-measure fields are used to set the measures.

You will use the third method.

6. Click the Measure Source dropdown arrow and click TWO_FIELDS.

This will enable both the From- and To-Measure Field input fields.

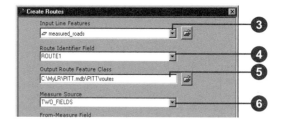

7. Click the From-Measure Field dropdown arrow and click BEGMP1.

8. Click the To-Measure Field dropdown arrow and click ENDMP1.

When you are writing to an existing feature dataset (as you are here), the spatial reference settings of that dataset will be applied to any new feature class. The exception to this rule is the m domain. Feature classes within the same feature dataset can have a different m domain. This accounts for the fact that different route feature classes might have different units of measure—for example, feet, meters, and miles. Whenever you create a route feature class in an existing feature dataset, you should always set an appropriate m domain. The spatial domain for a feature class or feature dataset cannot be changed. To learn more about the spatial reference, see later chapters in this book or *Building a Geodatabase*.

9. Click Environments to access the spatial reference m domain settings.

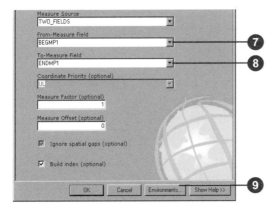

10. Expand Geodatabase Settings.

11. Click the Output M Domain dropdown arrow and click As Specified Below.

12. Type "-1000" for Min M and "10000" for Precision.

    The precision setting will ensure that your route measures will be accurate to four decimal places.

13. Click OK to close each dialog box.

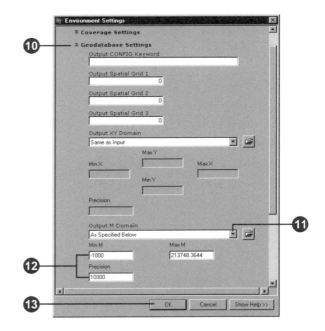

The tool's progress dialog box opens as the tool runs.

14. Click Close on the tool's progress dialog box when the process is finished.

Calibrating route data

Imagine that at some point in the future, the highway authority's road maintenance crew acquired a distance measuring instrument (DMI) to accurately record mileage information along the highways. For a sample set of highways, the crew went out and captured mileage information approximately every 1/10 of a mile. The results of this effort were stored as points in a shapefile, where the route and mileage information was stored as attributes.

In the next section of this tutorial, you will use the Calibrate Routes tool to adjust the measures of the routes you just created to match those of the points in the shapefile. The result will be written to a new feature class.

The Calibrate Routes tool is used to specify the input route feature class, the route identifier field, the input point feature class, the measure field, the methods used to set the route measures, and the output feature class.

1. Right-click the Calibrate Routes tool in the ArcToolbox Linear Referencing toolset, and click Open.

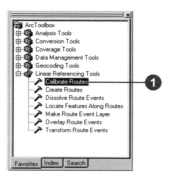

2. Type "C:\MyLR\PITT.mdb\PITT\routes" for the value of the Input Route Features parameter.

3. Click the Route Identifier Field dropdown arrow and click ROUTE1. The values in the Route Identifier Field uniquely identify each route.

4. Type "C:\MyLR\calibration_points.shp" for the value of the Input Point Features parameter.

5. Click the Point Identifier Field dropdown arrow and click ROUTE1. This is the common field, shared with the route feature class.

6. Click the Measure Field dropdown arrow and click MEASURE.

7. Type "C:\MyLR\PITT.mdb\PITT\routes_new" for the value of the Output Route Feature Class parameter.

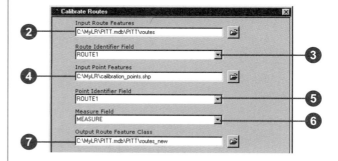

A tolerance can be specified to limit how far a calibration point can be from its route. Points outside the tolerance will not be used by the calibration process.

8. Click the Measure Calculation Method dropdown arrow and click DISTANCE.

9. Type "5" for the value of the Search Radius parameter. This is more than enough for the data that is being used here.

10. Click the Search Radius dropdown arrow and click Feet, to set the units to feet.

Again, you are writing to an existing feature dataset. All spatial reference settings will be borrowed from that spatial reference. It is a good habit to set the m domain whenever writing route data to a geodatabase.

11. Click Environments to access the spatial reference m domain settings.

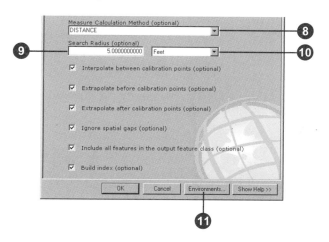

12. Expand Geodatabase Settings.

13. Click the Output M Domain dropdown arrow and click Same as Input.

You use the same m domain as the input route feature class. Note, however, that it is always a good practice to set the m domain.

14. Click OK to close each dialog box.

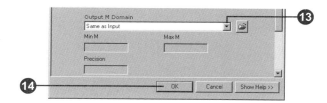

The tool's progress dialog box opens as the tool runs.

15. Click Close on the tool's progress dialog box when the process is finished.

In this exercise, you learned how to create a route feature class by merging input line features that shared a common identifier and how to adjust the route measures using measure information stored in a point shapefile. For more information on creating and calibrating route data, see Chapter 4, 'Creating route data'.

Exercise 3: Displaying and querying routes

In this exercise, you will add the route data you created in Exercise 2 to an existing map document and symbolize it. You will then

- Set the route identifier field.

- Add the Identify Route Locations tool to a toolbar.

- Identify route locations.

- Find route locations.

- Display route measure anomalies.

If you have not completed Exercise 2, open ArcCatalog. Within the Contents, delete PITT.mdb in your \MyLR folder and rename PITT_Results.mdb to PITT.mdb.

Opening an existing map document

To begin this exercise, you will start ArcMap and open an existing document.

1. Double-click a shortcut installed on your desktop or use the Programs list in your Start menu to start ArcMap.

2. In the Startup dialog box, choose to start using An existing map.

3. Double-click Browse for maps.

4. Click the Look in dropdown arrow in the Open dialog box and navigate to the folder where you copied the data for this tutorial (i.e., C:\MyLR).

5. Click Ex3.mxd to open the map in ArcMap.

6. Click Open.

This map contains the following layers in a data frame called Pitt County:

calibration_points	The points used in Exercise 2 to recalibrate the route measures
base_roads	All of the roads in Pitt County
city boundaries	The boundaries of the cities in Pitt County
county boundary	Pitt County boundary

The map currently displays the city boundaries and county boundary layers. Their check boxes are checked in the table of contents. The calibration_points layer is checked, but scale suppression has been set. It will only be visible when you zoom in to a scale beyond 1:25,000.

7. Check the box next to the base_roads layer in the table of contents.

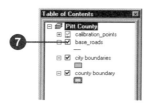

You will now see all of the roads in Pitt County. This includes roads not maintained by the highway authority. The roads maintained by the highway authority were written to the routes feature class.

Adding route data to your map

1. Click the Add Data button.

2. Click the Look in dropdown arrow and navigate to your \MyLR folder. Double-click PITT.mdb and double-click the PITT feature dataset.

3. Press the Ctrl key and select both the routes and routes_new feature classes.

4. Click Add.

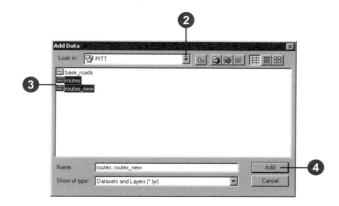

You will see the two new layers in the table of contents and also displayed in the ArcMap window.

Changing the display symbol

The colors and symbols in which ArcMap chose to display the routes layer might make it difficult to see where the route features are located. It is easy to change the colors and symbols used to display features in ArcMap.

1. Click the line symbol in the table of contents for the routes layer to display the Symbol Selector dialog box.

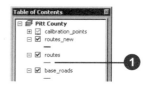

2. Scroll down until you find a symbol you like and click it.

3. Click OK. Your routes layer will be displayed with the symbol you chose.

4. Repeat steps 1 through 3 for the routes_new layer.

You can also open the Symbol Selector dialog box by right-clicking the layer in the table of contents, clicking Properties, and clicking the Symbology tab. To simply change the color of a symbol, right-click the symbol in the table of contents to display the color palette, click any color or More Colors. For more information on changing display symbols, see *Using ArcMap*.

You may have to click and drag the routes_new layer above routes in the table of contents to be able to see it.

Setting the Route Identifier field

Whenever route data is added to a map, ArcMap knows to expose some additional layer properties. One of these properties is the Route Identifier field. The contents of this field uniquely identify each route.

Setting the Route Identifier field is not required. Doing so, however, reduces the number of steps required to use many of the ArcMap Linear Referencing dialog boxes, tools, and wizards.

1. Right-click the routes layer in the table of contents and click Properties.

2. Click the Routes tab.

3. Click the Route Identifier dropdown arrow and click ROUTE1.

4. Click OK.

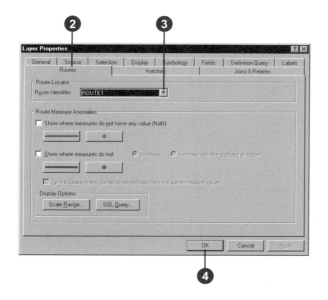

5. Repeat steps 1 through 4 for the routes_new layer.

Adding the Identify Route Locations tool

ArcMap gives you the ability to point to a route in a map and find the route identifier along with the measure value at that location. In this part of the exercise, you will use the Identify Route Locations tool to inspect the measures on the routes you created in Exercise 2.

The Identify Route Locations tool does not appear on any toolbar by default. You will have to add it to one.

1. Click Tools and click Customize.

2. Click the Commands tab.

3. Click Linear Referencing in the Categories list.

4. Drag and drop the Identify Route Locations tool to the toolbar of your choice, such as the Tools toolbar.

5. Click Close.

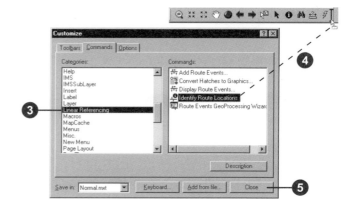

Identifying route locations

In ArcMap, a bookmark is a saved map location. A bookmark containing some of the calibration points used in Exercise 2 to recalibrate the routes has been created for you.

1. Click View, point to Bookmarks, and click Calibration Points.

When ArcMap moves to the saved location, the calibration points appear with labels that represent the measure values for each point. The reason they appear when the bookmark has been used is because scale suppression was set on the layer. For more information on scale suppression, see *Using ArcMap*.

2. Click the Identify Route Locations button.

3. Move the mouse pointer over one of the calibration points and click. Route locations from both the routes and routes_new layers will be identified.

4. Click the route node for each of the route layers.

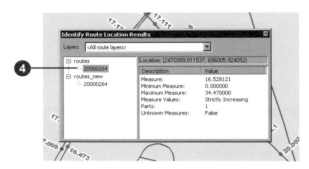

The numeric value listed for each of these nodes corresponds to the value stored in the Route Identifier field, which you set in a previous section of this exercise. Note that the measure value for the two routes differs. Note further that the measure value for the routes_new layer corresponds closely to the measure value of the calibration point you clicked—the closer you are to a calibration point, the closer the measure will be.

5. Right-click the route node for one of the layers and explore the context choices available to you.

6. Close the Identify Route Location Results window.

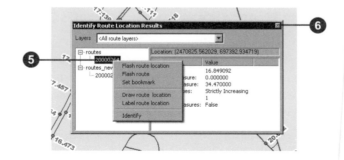

7. Uncheck the check box for the calibration_points layer in the table of contents to make it not visible. It will not be used any further in this exercise.

Finding route locations

In many linear referencing applications, you will discover that you will often need to find a location along a route. For example, you may need to find where an accident occurred along a highway. On a paper map, it is hard to find a route location. This is because route measures are typically not shown. In ArcMap, finding a route location is made easy.

1. Click the Find button on the ArcMap Tools toolbar.

2. Click the Route Locations tab to open the Find dialog box.

3. Click the Route Reference dropdown arrow and click routes_new.

Notice that the field listed in the Route Identifier dropdown arrow corresponds to the Route Identifier field you set previously in this exercise.

4. Click Load Routes.

5. Click the Route dropdown arrow and select 30000121.

This number is often a combination of many numeric fields and is meant to have no political, social, or economic meaning, so that it will not change over time.

6. Type "5" in the Location text box.

7. Click Find.

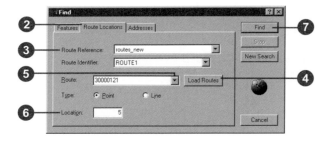

8. Right-click the route location that was found and explore the context choices available to you.

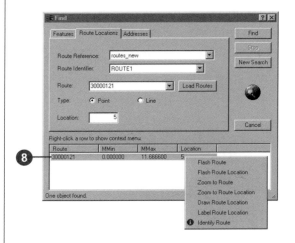

9. Close the Find dialog box.

Displaying route measure anomalies

In most linear referencing applications, route measure values are expected to follow a set of rules. For example, you might expect that route measures always increase over the course of a route. ArcMap has the ability to show you where route measures do not adhere to the behavior you expect. These are known as *route measure anomalies*.

1. Click the Full Extent button on the ArcMap Tools toolbar.

2. Right-click the routes layer in the table of contents and click Properties.

3. Click the Routes tab.

4. Check Show where measures do not increase.

5. Click the Line Symbol button and select a line symbol you like. Do the same for the marker symbol.

6. Click OK.

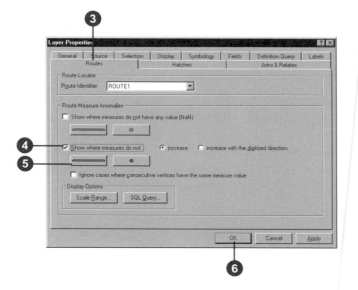

Remember that the routes feature class was created from the base_roads feature class in Exercise 2. There are a few digitizing and attribute errors that caused the measure anomalies to exist in the routes feature class. Route measure anomalies can be fixed with ArcMap route editing tools. For more information on route editing tools, see Chapter 6, 'Editing routes'.

Exercise 4: Displaying and querying route events

In this exercise, you will create a new event table that represents where injury accidents occurred along sections of poor-quality pavement. To do this, you will first use the Add Route Events dialog box to display the accident location and pavement quality event data on your map. You will then use the Select By Attributes dialog box to select the injury accidents and poor-quality pavement locations. You will use the Overlay Route Events tool to create a new event table whose records represent where injury accidents occurred along poor-quality pavement. Finally, you will add these events to the ArcMap display.

If you have not completed Exercise 2, open ArcCatalog. Within the Contents, delete PITT.mdb in your \MyLR folder and rename PITT_Results.mdb to PITT.mdb.

Opening an existing map document

To begin this exercise, you will start ArcMap and open an existing document.

1. Double-click a shortcut installed on your desktop or use the Programs list in your Start menu to start ArcMap.

2. Click File and click Open.

3. Click the Look in dropdown arrow in the Open dialog box and navigate to the location where you created the \MyLR folder.

4. Double-click Ex4.mxd. ArcMap opens the map.

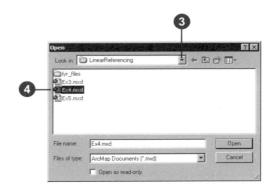

This map contains the following layers in a data frame called Pitt County:

routes_hwy	Shapefile copy of routes_new feature class you created in Exercise 2
county boundary	Pitt County boundary
accident	Point event table storing accident information
pavement	Line event table storing pavement information
base_roads	All of the roads in Pitt County

Displaying point events on your map

The accident table is a point event table. Point events occur at a precise point location along a route. In this section of the exercise, you will display the accident event data as a layer.

1. Click Tools and click Add Route Events.

2. Click the Route Reference dropdown arrow and click routes_hwy.

3. Click the Route Identifier dropdown arrow and click ROUTE1.

4. Click the Event Table dropdown arrow and click accident.

5. Click the Route Identifier dropdown arrow and click ROUTE1.

6. Click the Measure dropdown arrow and click MEASURE.

7. Click OK.

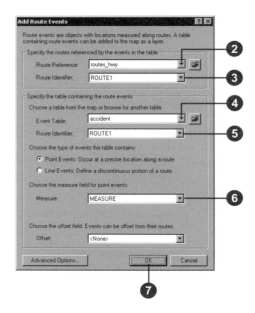

A new layer—accident Events—has been added to your map.

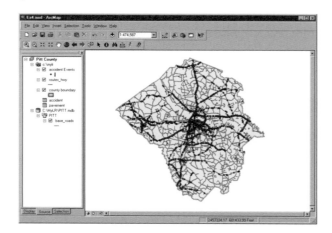

Displaying line events on your map

The pavement table is a line event table. Line events differ from point events in that they have two measure fields that define a portion of a route. The procedure for adding line events to your map is almost the same as adding point events.

1. Click Tools and click Add Route Events.

2. Click the Route Reference dropdown arrow and click routes_hwy.

3. Click the Route Identifier dropdown arrow and click ROUTE1.

4. Click the Event Table dropdown arrow and click pavement.

5. Click the Route Identifier dropdown arrow and click ROUTE1.

6. Click Line Events.

7. Click the From-Measure dropdown arrow and click BEGIN_MP.

8. Click the To-Measure dropdown arrow and click END_MP.

9. Click OK.

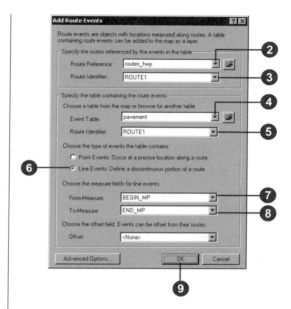

A new layer—pavement Events—has been added to your map.

You may have to use the zoom tool to zoom in on the map to see the pavement Events, or you could click and move the pavement Events layer to the top of the layer list in the table of contents.

Querying events

Layers based on an event table can be queried in many ways. They can be identified by clicking them, they can be selected by dragging a box or clicking them on the map, they can be selected by clicking them in an attribute table, and they can be selected using a Structured Query Language (SQL) expression. You will use the Select By Attributes dialog box to input expressions to select the event records needed for this exercise. Specifically, you will select injury accidents and poor quality pavement.

1. Click Selection and click Select By Attributes.

2. Click the Layer dropdown arrow and click accident Events.

3. Scroll down and double-click NUM_INJURY in the Fields list.

4. Click the greater than operator (>).

5. Click Get Unique Values.

6. Double-click 0 in the Unique Values list.

   "NUM_INJURY" > 0 should be the expression appearing in the text box.

7. Click Apply.

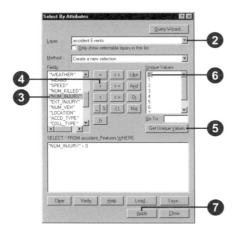

You will see a number of the features in the accident Events layer selected in the ArcMap display window.

8. Click the Layer dropdown arrow and click pavement Events in the Select By Attributes dialog box.

9. Type the following in the text box: "RATING" < 50

10. Click Apply.

11. Click Close.

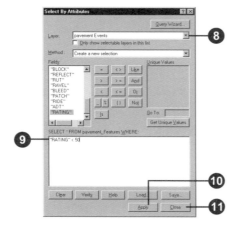

Now both the accident and pavement events are selected on your map. To see this more clearly, you may want to uncheck and check the accident Events and pavement Events layers in the table of contents.

In the next section of this exercise, you will use the Overlay Route Events tool in ArcToolbox to intersect the two event layers. The result will be a table that contains the injury accidents that happened on poor-quality pavement. All attributes from both inputs are maintained. First, however, you need to be sure that your geoprocessing results are automatically added to your display.

Setting geoprocessing results to display automatically

1. Click Tools and click Options.

2. Click the Geoprocessing tab.

3. Check Add results of geoprocessing operations to the display.

4. Click OK.

Intersecting event layers

1. Click the Show/Hide ArcToolbox button.

This opens the ArcToolbox window. You can dock and undock this window or move this window around the ArcMap window.

2. Expand the Linear Referencing Tools.

3. Right-click the Overlay Route Events tool and click Open.

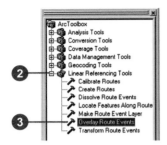

4. Click the Input Event Table dropdown arrow and click the accident Events layer.

NOTE: Because you selected an event layer, the Route Identifier Field, Event Type, and Measure Fields were set automatically. If you had selected an event table, you would be responsible for setting these parameters.

5. Click the Overlay Event Table dropdown arrow and click the pavement Events layer.

6. Click the Type of Overlay dropdown arrow and click INTERSECT. This will allow you to find the intersecting event layers.

7. Type "C:\MyLR\AccPav.dbf" for the value of the Output Event Table parameter.

You'll keep the remaining defaults.

8. Click OK.

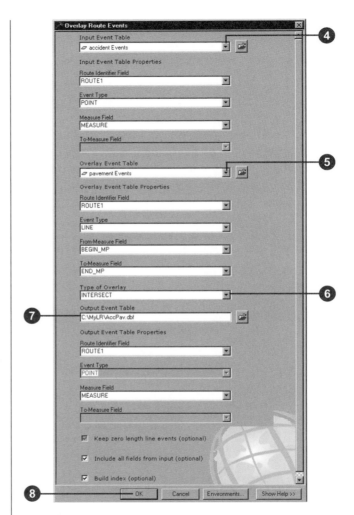

The tool's progress dialog box opens as the tool runs.

9. Click Close on the tool's progress dialog box when the process is finished.

10. The AccPav.dbf table is added to the ArcMap session. If you cannot see it in the table of contents, click the Source tab.

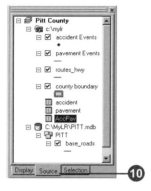

Displaying the intersected event results

At the beginning of this exercise, you used the Add Route Events dialog box (from the Main menu) to display the accident and pavement condition information as layers in your map. Another way to do this is to use the Make Route Event Layer tool (from ArcToolbox). When called from ArcCatalog, this tool creates a temporary, in-memory layer similar to the one you created in Exercise 2. When executed in ArcMap, the in-memory layer is added to the display.

1. Expand the Linear Referencing Tools in ArcToolbox.

2. Right-click the Make Route Event Layer tool and click Open.

3. Click the Input Route Features dropdown arrow and click the routes_hwy layer.

4. Click the Route Identifier Field dropdown arrow and click ROUTE1.

5. Click the Input Event Table dropdown arrow and click AccPav.

6. Click the Route Identifier Field dropdown arrow for the event table and click ROUTE1.

7. Click OK.

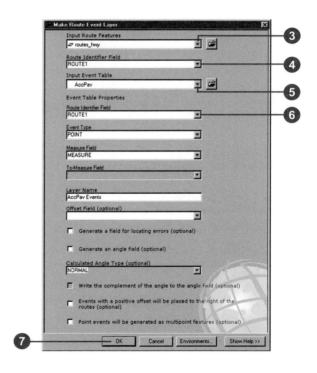

The AccPav Events layer is added to the table of contents.

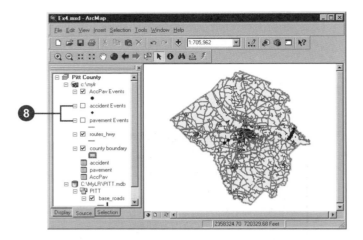

8. Uncheck the accident Events and pavement Events
   layers in the table of contents.

You will now see only the injury events that occurred along
poor quality pavement. Each of these new events has all
the attributes from both the accident and pavement tables.

For more information on the display and query of events or
the spatial analysis of events, see Chapter 5, 'Displaying
and querying routes and events', and Chapter 7, 'Creating
and editing event data'.

Exercise 5: Editing routes

There are a number of tools in ArcMap that make the interactive creation and editing of route measures easy. In this exercise, you will create a new route from a selected set of linear features and set its identifier. You will then convert the measures of this newly created route from feet to miles. Last, you will recalibrate the route using known measure values at specific locations on your map.

If you have not completed Exercise 2, open ArcCatalog. Within the Contents, delete PITT.mdb in your \MyLR folder and rename PITT_Results.mdb to PITT.mdb.

Opening an existing map document

In order to use this exercise, you must start ArcMap.

1. Double-click a shortcut installed on your desktop or use the Programs list in your Start menu to start ArcMap.

2. Click File and click Open.

3. Click the Look in dropdown arrow in the Open dialog box and navigate to the folder where you installed the data for this tutorial.

4. Double-click Ex5.mxd. ArcMap opens the map.

Adding route data to your map

You will use one of the route feature classes you created in Exercise 2 to complete this exercise.

1. Click the Add Data button.

ArcInfo and ArcEditor

2. Click the Look in dropdown arrow and navigate to your \MyLR folder. Double-click PITT.mdb and double-click the PITT feature dataset.

3. Click the routes_new feature class.

4. Click Add.

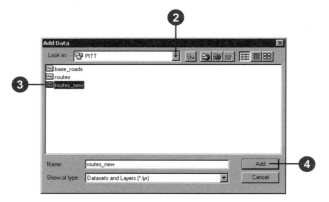

Adding the toolbars, editing, and setting the target feature class

The toolbars necessary to complete this exercise might not be visible.

1. Click the Editor Toolbar button to add the Editor toolbar to ArcMap.

2. Click the Editor menu, point to More Editing Tools, and click Route Editing.

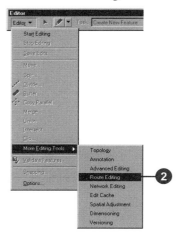

3. Click the Editor menu and click Start Editing.

4. Click the Target dropdown arrow on the Editor toolbar, and click routes_new.

Making a route from selected features

The highway authority has been informed that it will now be responsible for maintaining a road that it previously had not been maintaining. It is necessary, therefore, to select the appropriate features from the base_roads feature class and make a route in the routes_new feature class out of them.

The Make Route command creates a new route in the target feature class by merging a selected set of line features and setting the measure values. The selected line features do not need to be from the target feature class.

1. Click Selection and click Select By Attributes.

2. Click the Layer dropdown arrow and click base_roads.

3. Type the following in the text box:
   [FENAME] = 'Cornerstone Row'

If you're clicking in the field boxes to build the expression, you may need to click Complete List, under Unique sample values.

4. Click Apply.

5. Click Close.

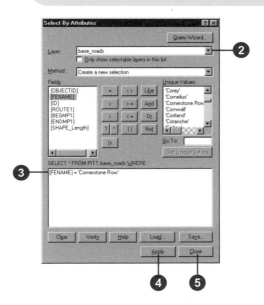

Nine features from the base_roads feature class are now selected.

6. Right-click the base_roads layer in the table of contents, point to Selection, and click Zoom To Selected Features.

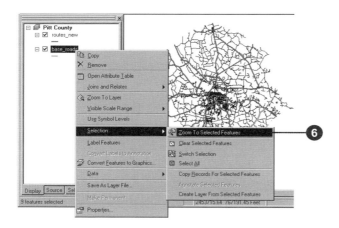

7. Right-click the base_roads feature class layer and click Open Attribute Table.

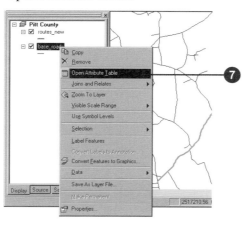

8. Click Selected to show only the selected records. You can also see the total number of selected records shown along the bottom of this window.

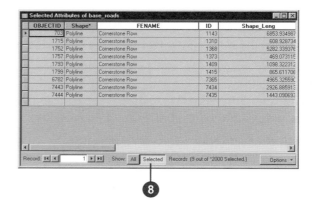

9. Close the Attributes table.

10. Click the Make Route button on the Route Editing toolbar.

11. Click the Start Point button.

The Make Route dialog box changes and lets you know you need to pick a route starting point.

12. Click the map near the upper-right corner of the selected set of features. This is where the output route's measures will begin.

The program tries to assist you by circling the endpoint it will select. As you move your mouse along the route, this point can change. This is useful because you do not need to select the exact spot on the route; just click on the display when the correct location is circled.

13. Click Make Route on the Make Route dialog box.

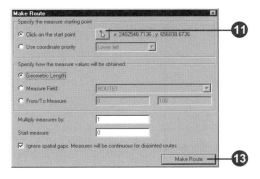

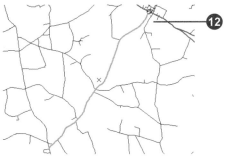

The new route will flash when it is being created. During the route creation process, the selected lines will be deselected, and the new route will be selected. This is so you can set the new route's attributes.

Setting the Route Identifier

Because the newly created route is selected, you can now set the route identifier. The route identifier uniquely identifies each route.

1. Click the Attributes button on the Editor toolbar.

2. Click the ROUTE1 Value and type "40001777".

3. Press Enter on your keyboard.

4. Close the Attributes dialog box.

ArcInfo and ArcEditor

Converting route measure units

When you created the new route, you accepted the default method for setting the route measures. This method accumulates the geometric length of the input line features and uses the length as the measure. Because the coordinate system of the feature class is State Plane Feet, the measures on the new route are in feet. However, the measures on all other routes in the feature class are in miles.

1. The newly created route should still be selected. If it is not, select it.

2. Click the Task dropdown arrow on the Editor toolbar and click Modify Feature.

The selected feature will now be loaded into the edit sketch.

3. Click the Sketch Properties button.

Note the size of the measure values (in column M).

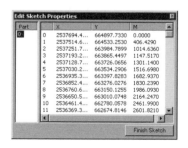

4. Close the Edit Sketch Properties dialog box.

5. Right-click anywhere over the edit sketch (you know you are over the line when the mouse pointer changes), point to Route Measure Editing, and click Apply Factor.

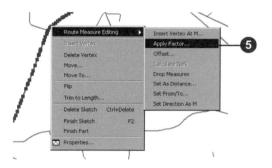

6. Type "0.00018939" in the Factor text box and press Enter on the keyboard. This converts feet to miles.

At this point, you have only made changes to the edit sketch, not the route feature.

7. Press F2 to finish the edit sketch. Alternately, right-click anywhere over the edit sketch and click Finish Sketch.

Your route measures are now in miles. You can verify this by double-clicking the selected route to bring it into the edit sketch, right-clicking anywhere over the sketch, and clicking Properties. Note that this is an alternate way to perform Steps 2 and 3.

Recalibrating a route

So far in this exercise, you have created a route and transformed its measures from feet to miles. Imagine that at some point the maintenance crew went out into the field and recorded the actual mileage for this new route. The mileage was captured every time the new route intersected with another route from the same feature class. In this section of the exercise, you will recalibrate the newly created route based on this mileage information.

1. The newly created route should still be selected. If it is not, select it.

2. Click the Editor menu and click Snapping.

This opens the Snapping Environment window, which is a dockable window.

3. Check the End check box next to the routes_new and base_roads layers.

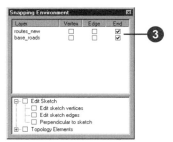

4. Close the Snapping Environment dialog box. It will not be used again in this exercise.

With the snapping environment set, you will be able to create calibration points that are snapped to the end vertex of the features in the routes_new layer, thereby ensuring accuracy of the route measures at the calibration points. Setting the snap environment, however, is not necessary for the Calibrate Route command to work.

5. Click the Task dropdown arrow and click Calibrate Route Feature.

6. Click the Calibrate Route button on the Route Editing toolbar.

ArcInfo and ArcEditor

The Calibrate Route dialog box is now on the screen, but it is empty. Your next task is to digitize the calibration points.

7. With the Calibrate Route dialog box open, click the Sketch tool on the Editor toolbar.

8. Click along the route at nine different places to create the calibration points. The locations of the calibration points are indicated in the graphic below.

9. Enter the New M values (see values in graphic below) for each calibration point by clicking each value in the column and typing the new value.

10. Click Calibrate Route.

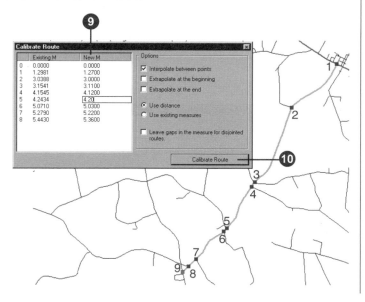

Saving your edits

Once you have completed the steps in this exercise, you can choose to save or discard your edits by stopping the edit session.

1. Click the Editor menu and click Stop Editing.

2. Click Yes to save your edits.

In this exercise, you first learned how to create a route from a selected set of line features. Next, you converted the route measures from feet to miles. Last, you learned how to recalibrate a route using calibration points you digitized on the map.

For more details about the route editing tools outlined here or for information on tools not discussed in this chapter, see Chapter 6, 'Editing routes'.

Linear referencing

3

Highways, city streets, railroads, rivers, pipelines, and water and sewer networks are all examples of linear features. *Linear features* typically have only one set of attributes. *Linear referencing*, however, provides you with an intuitive way to associate multiple sets of attributes to portions of linear features. With linear referencing, your ability to understand, maintain, and analyze linear features is greatly improved.

This chapter outlines the way linear features are modeled in ArcGIS. It then introduces you to what linear referencing is, explains why it is needed, and outlines the concepts necessary to develop linear referencing applications. Once you understand the concepts introduced in this chapter, you can refer to later chapters in this book to use the wide range of linear referencing functionality in ArcGIS.

The need for linear referencing

Geographic data is modeled in a number of ways: as a collection of features in *vector* format, as a grid of cells with spectral or attribute data in raster format, or as a set of triangulated points modeling a surface in triangulated irregular network (TIN) format.

Data having a discrete location with a defined shape and boundary is modeled using the vector format. In this format, data is represented by features, which are stored in feature classes. Every feature has a geometry associated with it. This geometry is stored in a special field typically called shape. A feature can have one of these types of geometries: point, multipoint, polyline, or polygon. Each geometry is composed of two-dimensional (x,y) or three-dimensional (x,y,z) geographic coordinates.

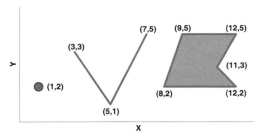

In the vector format, geographic data is stored as a feature that has a geometry type of point, multipoint, polyline, or polygon.

The vector format works well for modeling features with static characteristics, such as parcel boundaries, water bodies, and soil characteristics. Some applications, however, require the ability to model the relative location along various linear features, such as highways, city streets, railroads, rivers, pipelines, and water and sewer networks.

Because of this need, one-dimensional measuring systems, such as river mile and route milepost, have been devised. These systems simplify the recording of data by using a relative position along an already existing linear feature. That is, location is given in terms of a known linear feature and a position, or *measure*, along it. For example, route I-10, mile 23.2, uniquely identifies a position in geographic space without having to express it in x,y terms.

When data is linearly referenced, multiple sets of attributes can be associated with any portion of an existing linear feature, independent of its beginning and end. These attributes can be displayed, queried, edited, and analyzed without affecting the underlying linear feature's geometry.

The need to visually represent features on a map whose coordinates are not geographic but are recorded as a relative distance along another linear feature led to the development of dynamic segmentation. *Dynamic segmentation* is the process of displaying linearly referenced features on a map. For more information on dynamic segmentation, see Chapter 5, 'Displaying and querying routes and events'.

Storing features as relative locations

Locating a spatial feature along another linear feature would typically be done using a planar (two-dimensional) referencing system of x,y coordinates.

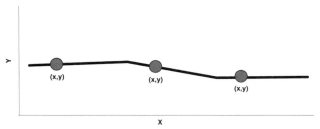

Locating accidents using x,y coordinates

This works well in some applications. In others, however, locations along linear features are referred to in terms of their distance from a known point. For example, it makes much more sense to record the location of an accident as occurring at "12 miles from the beginning of the interstate" rather than at "1659060.25, 1525238.97".

To determine a location along a linear feature, a system of measurement is required. When a measurement system is stored with a linear feature, any location along that linear feature can be expressed in terms of the measure values.

Locating accidents using measure values

In addition to making data more intuitive, storing data as a relative location along a linear feature has the added benefit of ensuring that spatial phenomena you know to be along a linear feature is mapped as such. For example, in the absence of an accurate basemap, locating accidents using x,y coordinates may end up displaying accidents that do not fall along the road network. This cannot happen if the accidents are stored as measurements along the linear features of the road network.

Segmented data

The *vector model* of data storage dictates that you must split a linear feature wherever its attribute values change. Certain linear features, however, have attributes that change frequently. The pavement condition of a road, for example, changes as pavement deteriorates and is subsequently repaired. To accurately reflect the changes in pavement condition, you will have to split some features and merge others.

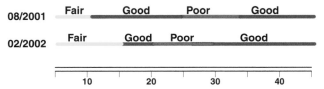

To attach attributes describing pavement quality, it is necessary to split a linear feature at several locations to reflect changes in data. Over time, pavement quality changes, requiring features to be split or merged.

Segmenting the linear features becomes more problematic when you need to store other attributes, such as traffic volumes, lane information, surface material, speed limits, and accident locations. Every time these attributes change, the road will need to be further subdivided. With all the required segmenting, it is evident that the linear features will be so subdivided that the data will be difficult, if not impossible, to maintain.

Accidents	●		●		●	
Lanes		2		4		
Material	Asphalt		Concrete		Asphalt	
Speed	45	35	45		55	
Quality	Fair	Good	Poor		Good	

10	20	30	40

Storing multiple sets of attributes for one feature is made possible using linear referencing.

ArcGIS uses route event tables to store linearly referenced attributes. Event rows are composed of a route identifier, measure values indicating a location, and one or more attributes describing the location. For more information on route event tables, see 'Route locations and route events' in this chapter.

Because events simply reference measure locations along linear features, they are edited and maintained independently of the linear features. For more information on maintaining event data, see Chapter 7, 'Creating and editing event data'.

Routes and measures

When linearly referenced features in ArcGIS are referred to, the terms routes and route events are used. A *route* is any linear feature, such as a city street, highway, river, or pipe, that has a unique identifier and a measurement system. This measurement system defines discrete locations along the linear feature. For more information on route events, see 'Route locations and route events' in this chapter.

Linear feature with measures — Unique identifier

A route is a linear feature with a unique identifier and a measurement system.

A collection of routes with a common system of measurement can be stored in a single *feature class*—such as a set of all highway routes in a county. In a geodatabase, many feature classes containing routes can be stored in a single *feature dataset*. For example, a state's department of transportation (DOT) might maintain a feature dataset with feature classes for milepost routes, reference marker routes, and so on.

- NYSDOT.mdb
  - R1Route
    - CoupletRoute
    - MileptRoute
    - OffstateRoute
    - R1Route_Topology
    - ReferenceLine
    - ReferencePoint
    - RefmkrRoute
    - ThruwayRoute

A feature dataset can have multiple feature classes that store routes.

Linear features and, therefore, routes are stored in a feature class whose geometry type is a polyline. A *polyline* is an ordered collection of paths that can be connected or disjointed. Polylines are used to represent such things as roads, rivers, and contours.

Polyline with one path   Polyline with multiple, connected paths   Polyline with multiple, disjointed paths

A polyline is an ordered collection of paths that can be connected or disjointed.

Polylines can have a measurement system stored with their geometry. Instead of being a collection of segments with x,y coordinates, a measured polyline's segments have x,y and m (measure) or x,y,z and m values. When a measure value is unknown, it is listed as NaN (not a number).

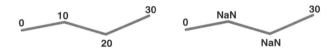

Polylines can have a measurement system stored with their geometry. Measures can be unknown (NaN).

It is important to note that although many applications use measures to represent increasing distances along a linear feature, measure values can arbitrarily increase, remain constant, or decrease.

Measure values are independent of the *coordinate system* of a feature class. That is, the measure values are not required to be in the same units as the feature class's x,y coordinates. For example, features stored in a feature class whose coordinate system is *Universal Transverse Mercator (UTM)* meters might have measure values stored in feet or miles.

Route locations and route events

A *route location* describes a discrete location along a route (point) or a portion of a route (line). A point route location uses only a single measure value to describe a discrete location along a route. An example of a point route location is "mile 3.2 on the I-91." A line route location uses both a from- and a to-measure value to describe a portion of a route. "Mile 2 to mile 4 on the I-91" is an example of a linear route location.

When route locations—and their associated attributes—are stored in a table, they are known as *route events* or simply *events*. Events are organized into tables based on a common theme. For example, five event tables containing information on speed limits, year of resurfacing, present condition, signs, and accidents can reference highway routes.

Route event tables

Because there are two types of route locations, there are two types of route event tables: point and line.

A *route event table*, at a minimum, consists of two fields: a route identifier and a measure location. The route identifier field is a numeric or character value used to identify the route to which an event belongs. A measure location is either one or two fields that describe the positions along the route at which the event occurs. These values can be defined as any numeric item.

An event table can be any type of table that ArcGIS supports. This includes INFO™, dBASE®, geodatabase tables, delimited text files, and database management system (DBMS) tables accessed via an Object Linking and Embedding Database (OLE DB) connection.

Point events

Point events occur at a precise point location along a route. Accident locations along highways, signals along rail lines, bus stops along bus routes, and pumping stations along pipelines are all examples of point events. Point events use a single measure value to describe their location.

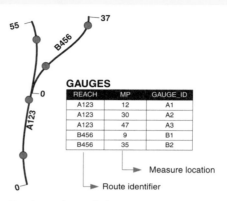

GAUGES

REACH	MP	GAUGE_ID
A123	12	A1
A123	30	A2
A123	47	A3
B456	9	B1
B456	35	B2

Measure location

Route identifier

Events are located along a route using their route location information. Here, point events representing flow gauges along river reaches are shown.

Line events

Line events describe portions of routes. Pavement quality, salmon spawning grounds, bus fares, pipe widths, and traffic volumes are all examples of line events. Line events use two measure values to describe their location.

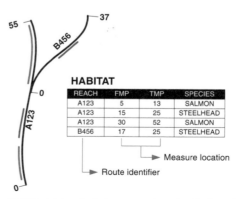

HABITAT

REACH	FMP	TMP	SPECIES
A123	5	13	SALMON
A123	15	25	STEELHEAD
A123	30	52	SALMON
B456	17	25	STEELHEAD

Measure location

Route identifier

Events are located along a route using their route location information. Here, line events representing fish habitats along river reaches are shown.

Linear referencing and topology

Within an organization, there may be many departments that use route event data. Each department will collect event data using the route measurement system that best suits its needs. Within a state DOT, for example, the safety department might collect accident location events using a reference marker system of measurement, while the maintenance department might collect pavement quality information using a milepost system of measurement. Each system is known as a *linear referencing method*.

A route in ArcGIS can only store one system of measurement. In many organizations, therefore, there is a need to maintain multiple route feature classes—one for each linear referencing method. The ability to manage these feature classes in an integrated fashion is critical.

In GIS technology, *topology* is the model used to describe how features share geometry. It is also the mechanism for establishing and maintaining topological relationships between features and feature classes. ArcGIS implements topology through a set of validation rules that define how features share geographic space and a set of editing tools that work with features that share geometry in an integrated fashion.

By defining a topology, organizations can achieve the data integration between route feature classes they require. For more information on topology, see *Building a Geodatabase* and *Editing in ArcMap*.

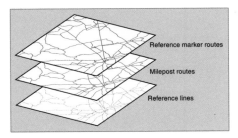

A topology facilitates the use of multiple linear referencing methods.

Creating route data

4

Before embarking on any linear referencing project, you will need route data. This data may not exist, may exist but without the appropriate measure system defined, or may exist in a format you do not wish to use.

ArcGIS supports routes in three formats: coverage, shapefile, and geodatabase. ArcCatalog and ArcToolbox provide you with the tools necessary to create, calibrate, and migrate route data from one supported format to another.

In this chapter, you will learn how to:

- Create new route feature classes.

- Create route feature classes from existing lines.

- Calibrate routes using points.

- Migrate routes from one format to another.

Route data

A *route* is a linear feature that has a unique identifier and measurement system stored with it. Routes can be stored in coverages, shapefiles, personal geodatabases, and ArcSDE® geodatabases.

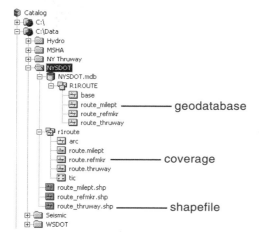

Routes can be stored in coverages, shapefiles, and geodatabase feature classes.

ArcCatalog and ArcToolbox contain tools for creating route data in shapefiles and geodatabases. In addition to the ability to create empty route feature classes for later digitizing or importing, there are tools for creating routes by merging existing line features, calibrating route data with points, and migrating route data from one format to another. When a route feature class is stored in a geodatabase, there are special storage considerations. Some of these are general geodatabase considerations that can be read about in *Building a Geodatabase*. Others are particular to linear referencing applications and will be explained further in this section.

There are tools for creating routes in coverages, but they will not be discussed in this chapter. ArcInfo Workstation remains the best place to create coverage route data. For more information on creating coverage route data, see the ArcInfo Workstation online Help.

Merging linear features to create routes

It is possible to create routes by merging linear features that share a common identifier. There are two scenarios for how the route measures will be set:

- Measure values for the input features are not known.
- Measure values for the input features are known.

Measure values are not known

When route measure values are not known, they can be generated either by accumulating the digitized length or by accumulating a numeric attribute value of the input features. If you choose to use digitized length, the units of the output route measures will be the same as the output coordinate system (e.g., feet or meters). If you choose to use a numeric attribute, the output route measures can be in any units you want.

When routes are created in this manner, you control the direction measures are assigned to the routes by specifying the coordinate priority of the starting measure. The coordinate priority can be upper left, upper right, lower left, or lower right. These options are determined by placing the minimum bounding rectangle around the input features that are going to be merged to create one route.

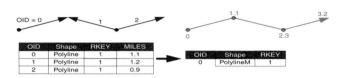

OID	Shape	RKEY	MILES
0	Polyline	1	1.1
1	Polyline	1	1.2
2	Polyline	1	0.9

OID	Shape	RKEY
0	PolylineM	1

Measure values are obtained by accumulating the values in the MILES field. Note that the digitized direction of the input features does not matter because a starting priority is given. In this example, the starting priority is lower left.

Routes with multiple, disjointed parts are supported. A route representing a road, for example, might have the same name on either side of a river. For situations like this, you can choose to ignore spatial gaps between parts when creating routes. If you choose to ignore spatial gaps, route measures will be continuous when a disjointed route is created. If you want the spatial gap incorporated in the measures, the gap distance is the straight-line distance between the endpoints of the parts. The units of the gap will be that of the output coordinate system, which may or may not be the same as the measure units.

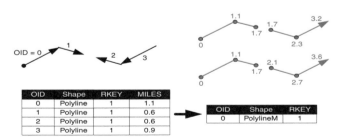

OID	Shape	RKEY	MILES
0	Polyline	1	1.1
1	Polyline	1	0.6
2	Polyline	1	0.6
3	Polyline	1	0.9

OID	Shape	RKEY
0	PolylineM	1

When creating disjointed routes, you can choose to have the measures be continuous or discontinuous. In this example, the starting priority is lower left.

Measure values are known

When measure information already exists as attributes of the input linear features, it is possible to create routes that inherit this measure information. For example, two fields may exist that store from- and to-mile information.

When using this method, it is important to orient each input linear feature in the direction of increasing measure to prevent routes that have measures that do not always increase.

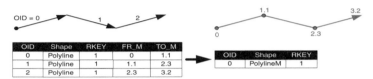

OID	Shape	RKEY	FR_M	TO_M
0	Polyline	1	0	1.1
1	Polyline	1	1.1	2.3
2	Polyline	1	2.3	3.2

OID	Shape	RKEY
0	PolylineM	1

Measure values are obtained by using the values in the FR_M and TO_M fields. Note that the digitized direction of the input features determines the direction of the output route.

Calibrating route measures using points

When route measures are inaccurate, events will not be located properly. A route representing a highway, for example, might be 10.5 miles long. A bend in the highway might have its measure value set to 6.1 miles. In reality, however, the bend in the highway occurs at mile 6.5. Events on this route, especially near the bend, will be located incorrectly.

It is possible to adjust route measures to correspond with known measure locations using a procedure called calibration. *Calibration* adjusts route measures by reading measure information stored as an attribute in a point feature class. Each point falls on the particular route it calibrates or within a given radius. Many points may be used to calibrate a single route.

During the calibration process, a new vertex is created where the calibration points intersect the route. The measure value on these new vertices corresponds to the measure value stored as a point attribute. The measure values on other preexisting route vertices can be interpolated and/or extrapolated.

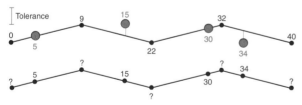

The calibration process creates a new vertex for every point within the specified tolerance. The measure at each new vertex will correspond to the point's measure value. You control whether the remaining vertices will have their measure interpolated or extrapolated.

Both whole and partial routes can be calibrated. You can choose to interpolate between the input points, extrapolate before the input points, extrapolate after the input points, or use any combination of these three methods.

In order for the measure value on a vertex to be interpolated or extrapolated, a calibration ratio is needed. There are two ways this ratio can be determined. The first method uses the shortest path distance between the input points.

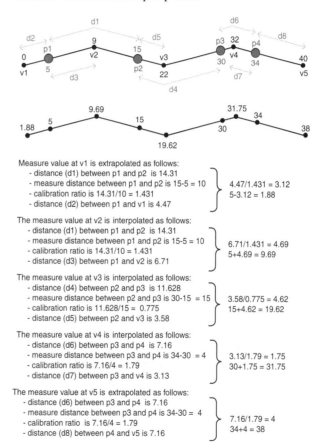

Measure value at v1 is extrapolated as follows:
- distance (d1) between p1 and p2 is 14.31
- measure distance between p1 and p2 is 15-5 = 10
- calibration ratio is 14.31/10 = 1.431
- distance (d2) between p1 and v1 is 4.47

4.47/1.431 = 3.12
5-3.12 = 1.88

The measure value at v2 is interpolated as follows:
- distance (d1) between p1 and p2 is 14.31
- measure distance between p1 and p2 is 15-5 = 10
- calibration ratio is 14.31/10 = 1.431
- distance (d3) between p1 and v2 is 6.71

6.71/1.431 = 4.69
5+4.69 = 9.69

The measure value at v3 is interpolated as follows:
- distance (d4) between p2 and p3 is 11.628
- measure distance between p2 and p3 is 30-15 = 15
- calibration ratio is 11.628/15 = 0.775
- distance (d5) between p2 and v3 is 3.58

3.58/0.775 = 4.62
15+4.62 = 19.62

The measure value at v4 is interpolated as follows:
- distance (d6) between p3 and p4 is 7.16
- measure distance between p3 and p4 is 34-30 = 4
- calibration ratio is 7.16/4 = 1.79
- distance (d7) between p3 and v4 is 3.13

3.13/1.79 = 1.75
30+1.75 = 31.75

The measure value at v5 is extrapolated as follows:
- distance (d6) between p3 and p4 is 7.16
- measure distance between p3 and p4 is 34-30 = 4
- calibration ratio is 7.16/4 = 1.79
- distance (d8) between p4 and v5 is 7.16

7.16/1.79 = 4
34+4 = 38

The calibration ratio can be determined using the shortest path distance between the input points.

The second method uses the existing measure distance between the input points. This second method is useful when the length to measure ratio on the input route is not consistent and you are using the calibration process to fine-tune a route's measures.

When calibrating disjointed routes, you may choose to ignore the distance of the spatial gap between the parts. If you choose to ignore spatial gaps, route measures will be continuous. If you want the spatial gap incorporated in the measures, the gap distance is the straight-line distance between the endpoints of the parts. The units of the gap will be that of the output coordinate system, which may or may not be the same as the measure units. Ignoring spatial gaps is only a valid choice when using the shortest path distance method of calibration.

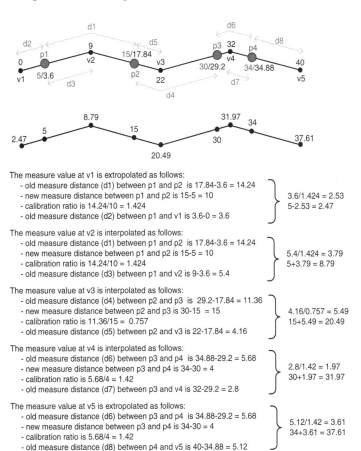

The measure value at v1 is extropolated as follows:
  - old measure distance (d1) between p1 and p2 is 17.84-3.6 = 14.24
  - new measure distance between p1 and p2 is 15-5 = 10
  - calibration ratio is 14.24/10 = 1.424
  - old measure distance (d2) between p1 and v1 is 3.6-0 = 3.6

3.6/1.424 = 2.53
5-2.53 = 2.47

The measure value at v2 is interpolated as follows:
  - old measure distance (d1) between p1 and p2 is 17.84-3.6 = 14.24
  - new measure distance between p1 and p2 is 15-5 = 10
  - calibration ratio is 14.24/10 = 1.424
  - old measure distance (d3) between p1 and v2 is 9-3.6 = 5.4

5.4/1.424 = 3.79
5+3.79 = 8.79

The measure value at v3 is interpolated as follows:
  - old measure distance (d4) between p2 and p3 is 29.2-17.84 = 11.36
  - new measure distance between p2 and p3 is 30-15 = 15
  - calibration ratio is 11.36/15 = 0.757
  - old measure distance (d5) between p2 and v3 is 22-17.84 = 4.16

4.16/0.757 = 5.49
15+5.49 = 20.49

The measure value at v4 is interpolated as follows:
  - old measure distance (d6) between p3 and p4 is 34.88-29.2 = 5.68
  - new measure distance between p3 and p4 is 34-30 = 4
  - calibration ratio is 5.68/4 = 1.42
  - old measure distance (d7) between p3 and v4 is 32-29.2 = 2.8

2.8/1.42 = 1.97
30+1.97 = 31.97

The measure value at v5 is extropolated as follows:
  - old measure distance (d6) between p3 and p4 is 34.88-29.2 = 5.68
  - new measure distance between p3 and p4 is 34-30 = 4
  - calibration ratio is 5.68/4 = 1.42
  - old measure distance (d8) between p4 and v5 is 40-34.88 = 5.12

5.12/1.42 = 3.61
34+3.61 = 37.61

The calibration ratio can be determined using the measure distance between the input points.

Special considerations for geodatabases

When you create a new standalone feature class or a feature class in a new feature dataset, you must specify a spatial reference. The spatial reference for a feature class contains its coordinate system—for example, geographic, UTM, and State Plane—and the spatial domains—x,y,z, and m. For more information on spatial references, see *Building a Geodatabase*.

You need to choose appropriate x,y,m, and perhaps z domains when creating route feature classes because they describe the maximum extent to which data can grow. For example, if you create a feature class with a minimum m-value of 0 and a precision of 1,000, none of the routes in the feature class will be able to have measures that are less than 0. Furthermore, all route measures will be accurate to three decimal places (a precision of 1,000 implies accuracy to three decimal places). Similar considerations apply to the x,y, and z domains.

All feature classes in a feature dataset share a common spatial reference. This means that the domains are shared as well. The exception to the rule is the m domain. Feature classes within the same feature dataset can have a different m domain. This is to account for the fact that different route feature classes might have different units of measure—for example, feet, meters, and miles. Whenever you create a route feature class in an existing feature dataset, you should always set an appropriate m domain.

Choosing an appropriate m domain

However route data is created, one important goal is to preserve measure accuracy. When data is stored in a geodatabase, all numeric values are converted to integers. Because of this, converting data to and from integer space can sacrifice measure accuracy if inappropriate m domain values are used.

To determine an appropriate m domain, you need to know both the route storage units and the route measure units. The route storage units reflect how accurately the route data was collected. For example, route measure data may be accurate to the foot, meter, or even decimeter level.

The route measure units refer to the units in which route locations are reported. For example, they may be feet, meters, miles, and so on. Route measure units have nothing to do with how accurately the route's data was collected and stored.

Precision is the multiplier that scales measure units into storage units. The lowest precision value you should use is the route measure units divided by the storage units. For example, if the route measure units are kilometers and there is meter-level accuracy, the lowest precision value you should use is 1,000. This is because there are 1,000 meters in a kilometer, and $1/0.001$ equals 1,000. Further, if the route measure units are miles and there is accuracy to the foot, the lowest precision you should use is 5,280 (there are 5,280 feet per mile).

Suppose you have a route feature class in which the route measure units are kilometer and the route storage units are accurate to the meter level. Further suppose that this route feature class has an m domain in which the measure minimum is -1,000 and the measure precision is 100, which is incorrect. If a new route is created in this feature class and its measure values are set to range between 0 and 1,324.526, the following diagram illustrates that the accuracy of the route's measures is not maintained when the route is stored and subsequently retrieved from the geodatabase. Note that the same process happens for every measure value on the route.

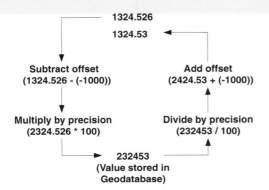

When an incorrect measure precision is used, measure accuracy can be lost on a round-trip to the geodatabase.

If the route feature class has an appropriate m precision of 1,000, the measure accuracy of the route is maintained on a round-trip to the geodatabase.

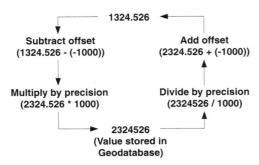

When a correct measure precision is used, measure accuracy is maintained on a round-trip to the geodatabase.

It is often a good idea to use a precision that is greater than the calculated value to allow for the future storage of more accurate data. In most cases this is not a problem, but be aware that there is a trade-off between precision and the range of measure in which values can be stored. The higher the precision value that is used, the smaller the range of measure values that routes can have.

Grid size

Another consideration regarding geodatabase feature classes is the grid size of the spatial index. The spatial index is used to quickly locate features that match the criteria of a spatial search.

For most data, only a single grid size is required. Because feature size is an important factor in determining an optimum grid size, data that contains features of very different sizes may require additional grid sizes so larger features can be queried faster. Feature classes in ArcSDE geodatabases may have up to three grid sizes. Each grid size must be at least three times the previous grid size. For a more detailed discussion of spatial indexes and grid sizes, see the ArcSDE Administration Guide PDF file and the ArcSDE Configuration and Tuning Guide for <DBMS> PDF file.

When creating a new route feature class from scratch, a single default grid size of 1,000 will be used. This value should always be changed to an appropriate value.

When merging lines to create routes, calibrating route measures with points, or migrating route data to a geodatabase, an attempt to borrow grid size settings from the input will be made. If grid settings cannot be borrowed, default ones will be calculated for you. Borrowed or default grid settings will not always be appropriate. For example, when merging lines to create routes, borrowed or default grid settings will be based on the input features. Because (potentially) many lines will be merged to create a single route, a grid size based on smaller features might not be appropriate for larger ones.

Another consideration to make when merging lines to create routes, calibrating route measures with points, or migrating route data to a geodatabase is that borrowed or default grid settings are specified in the same units as the coordinate system of the input data. If the output data is to be written to a different coordinate system, grid settings need to be specified in the units of the output coordinate system. For example, if the input feature class has a geographic coordinate system and its units are decimal degrees, the default grid size may be 10. If the output coordinate system is set to be UTM meters, the default grid size should be set to a value suitable for new units, such as 10,000.

If inappropriate grid settings are used, an error stating that the grid size is too small may occur when storing features in a feature class, or you may experience poor spatial search performance.

Creating route feature classes

You create new route feature classes in ArcCatalog. When creating a route feature class, you must define the geometry field's geometry type to be polyline and indicate that it be able to store measure values. You also need to add a route identifier field. This field uniquely identifies each route.

When creating a route feature class in a geodatabase, you must also define the spatial reference. Note that if you are creating a feature class in a preexisting feature dataset, you need only set the m domain. This is because all feature classes in a feature dataset share a common spatial reference, which was created when the feature dataset was created. The m domain, however, can be different for each feature class. This is because route feature classes in a feature dataset often have different units of measure—for example, feet, meters, and miles.

When creating a shapefile that will store routes, you may choose to define the coordinate system later. It will be classified as Unknown until that time. ►

Creating a new standalone feature class to store routes

1. Right-click the geodatabase in the Catalog tree in which you want to create a new route feature class, point to New, then click Feature Class.

2. Type a name for the new feature class. To create an alias for this feature class, type the alias.

3. Click This feature class will store ESRI simple features (e.g., point, line, polygon).

4. Click Next. ►

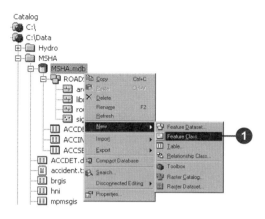

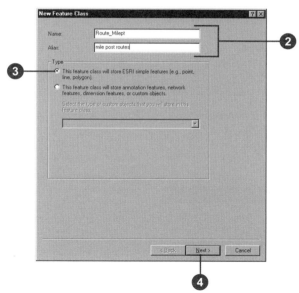

The process of defining a shapefile's attributes is separate from creating the shapefile itself. To create the route identifier plus all other fields, you need to right-click in the Catalog tree and click Properties to define the attributes. Note that because a shapefile must contain at least one field, the integer field ID has already been added. Add the appropriate fields to the shapefile, then delete the default field.

Tip

Using another feature class as a template

When creating a new feature class in a geodatabase, you can use another feature class as a template. Click Import, navigate to the feature class whose field definitions you want to copy, then click OK. You can edit the field names and types as required.

See Also

For details about using configuration keywords with ArcSDE, see the ArcSDE Configuration and Tuning Guide for <DBMS> PDF file.

If your geodatabase does not use ArcSDE, skip to step 6.

5. Click Use configuration keyword and click the keyword you want to use if you want to create a feature class with a custom storage keyword.

6. Click Next.

7. Click the SHAPE field in the Field Name column.

8. Click the field next to Alias, in Field Properties, and enter an alias name to be used for the SHAPE field.

9. Click the field next to Allow NULL values, click the dropdown arrow, then click No to prevent null shapes from being stored.

10. Click the field next to Geometry Type, click the dropdown arrow, then click Line for the feature's type.

11. Click the field next to the grids and type the grid values to set the spatial index grid parameters for the feature class.

12. Click the field next to Contains M values, click the dropdown arrow, then click Yes.

13. Click the Spatial Reference Properties button. ▶

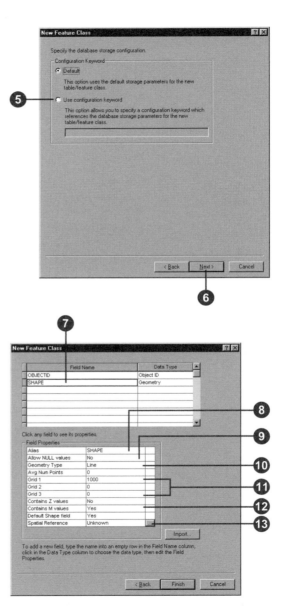

Precision

The size of a spatial domain (X/Y, Z, or M) is dependent on the value of precision. When the precision is changed, the maximum value for the domain will change to fit the size of the extent. Similarly, when the maximum value is changed, the precision will change to fit the extent.

See Also

For details on how to create a new coordinate system and for important information about spatial references and how they affect your data, see Building a Geodatabase.

14. Click Select, Import, or New to set the feature class's coordinate system.

15. Click the X/Y Domain tab.

16. Type the Min X and Precision values for the X/Y Domain.

17. Click the M Domain tab.

18. Type the Min and Precision values for the M Domain.

19. Click OK. ▶

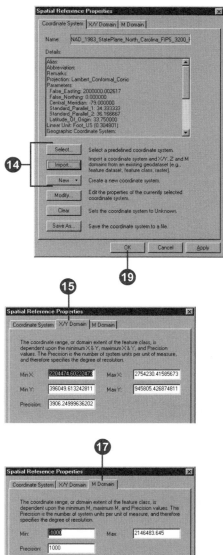

Creating a route feature class in an existing feature dataset

The process of creating a route feature class in an existing feature dataset is similar to that of creating a standalone route feature class. However, steps 13 through 15 are not valid because all feature classes in a feature dataset share a common spatial reference, which was created when the feature dataset was created and cannot be changed. The exception is the m domain, which you should always set.

Tip

Creating an index on the route identifier field

It is recommended that you create an attribute index on the route identifier field. This index will improve dynamic segmentation performance.

See Also

For more information on creating a field index in a feature class, see Building a Geodatabase.

See Also

For more information on creating a feature class in a feature dataset, see Building a Geodatabase.

20. Click the next blank row in the Field Name column to add the route identifier field to the feature class and type a new field name—for example, Route_ID.

21. Click in the Data Type column next to the new field's name and select its data type.

22. Enter or select the properties for the Field Properties.

23. Repeat steps 20 through 22 until fields for the feature class have been defined.

24. Click Finish.

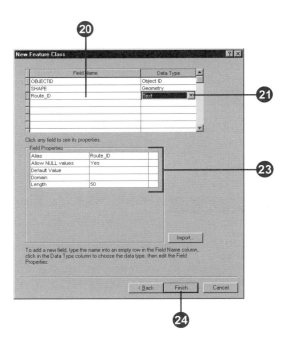

See Also

For more information on creating shapefiles, see Using ArcCatalog.

Creating a new shapefile to store routes

1. Right-click the folder in the Catalog tree in which you want to create a new shapefile, point to New, then click Shapefile.

2. Type a name for the new shapefile.

3. Click the Feature Type dropdown arrow and click Polyline.

4. Check Coordinates will contain M values.

5. Click Edit to define the shapefile's coordinate system.

   When you are finished setting the shapefile's coordinate system (step 7), you will be returned to this dialog box. ▶

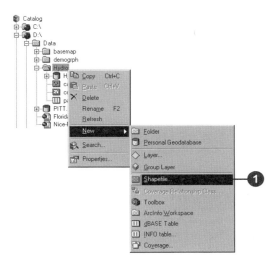

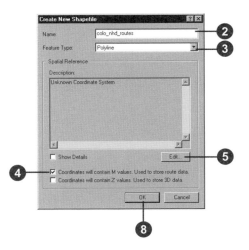

6. Click Select, Import, or New to set the shapefile's spatial reference.

7. Click OK.

8. Click OK to create the shapefile.

9. Right-click the feature class in the Catalog tree and click Properties.

   This will open the Properties dialog box, so you can add the route identifier field to the shapefile. ▶

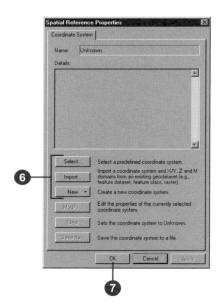

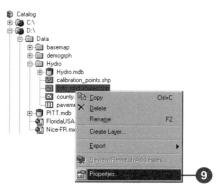

Tip

Deleting the default ID field

The integer field ID is a default field and can be deleted once another field has been added to the shapefile.

10. Click the Fields tab.

11. Click the next blank row in the Field Name column and type a name for the route identifier field.

12. Click in the Data Type column next to the new field's name and click its data type.

13. Click in the Field Properties list and type the properties for the new field.

14. Repeat steps 10 through 13 until all the shapefiles' fields have been defined.

15. Click OK.

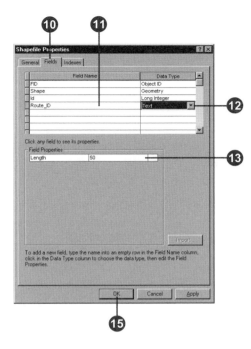

ArcInfo and ArcEditor

Creating routes from existing lines

You create routes from existing lines using the Create Routes tool in the Linear Referencing toolbox in ArcToolbox.

The input feature classes can be any supported format. This includes coverage, shapefile, personal and enterprise geodatabase, and CAD data.

The linear features used as input, sharing a common identifier, are merged to create a single route. As the input linear features are merged, the route measures are determined in one of three ways:

- The geometric lengths of the input features are used to accumulate the measures.

- A value stored in a measure field is used to accumulate the measures.

- The values stored in from- and to-measure fields are used to set the measures.

With the first two options, you choose whether the output routes will have continuous measures when there are disjointed parts.

Also with the first two options, you control the direction measures are assigned to the routes by specifying the ▶

1. Click the Show/Hide ArcToolbox button on the Standard toolbar to show ArcToolbox.

2. Expand the Linear Referencing Tools.

3. Double-click the Create Routes tool.

4. Type the Input Line Features filename and path, click the Browse button to select it, or click the dropdown arrow to select a layer.

5. Click the Route Identifier Field dropdown arrow and click the route identifier field.

6. Type the Output Route Feature Class filename and path or click the Browse button to specify the output location.

7. Click the Measure Source dropdown arrow and click the option in which you want the output route measures to be obtained.

8. For point events, click the Measure Field dropdown arrow and click the measure field.

   For line events, click the From-Measure Field dropdown arrow and click the from-measure field. Click the To-Measure Field dropdown arrow and click the to-measure field. ▶

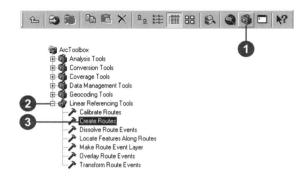

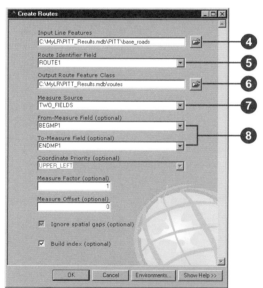

coordinate priority of the starting measure. The coordinate priority can be upper left, upper right, lower left, or lower right. These options are determined by placing the minimum bounding rectangle around the input features that are going to be merged to create one route.

The output routes can be written to a shapefile or a geodatabase feature class. When writing to a geodatabase, you should always have an appropriate m domain set. If it is not set, a default m domain will be calculated for you, but this might not accurately reflect your data.

Tip

Set environment settings for multiple operations

When using the same environment settings for multiple geoprocessing operations, set them at the application level. These environment settings can be accessed through Tools | Options on the Geoprocessing tab.

Tip

Create Routes Wizard

The Create Routes Wizard is available in ArcCatalog via the Customize dialog box. You can add it to your context window or toolbars.

9. Optionally, click the Coordinate Priority dropdown arrow and click a coordinate priority. This becomes active when a Measure Source is LENGTH or ONE_FIELD.

10. Click Environments.

11. Expand Geodatabase Settings.

12. Click the Output M Domain dropdown arrow and click As Specified Below.

13. Type a value for Min M and Precision.

14. Click OK to close each dialog box.

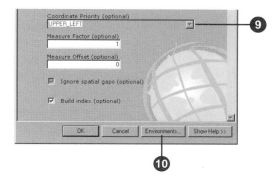

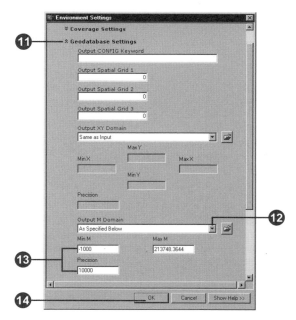

ArcInfo and ArcEditor

Calibrating routes with points

When calibrating routes with points, you can choose to exclude routes without any associated calibration points from the output.

The calibration of whole or partial routes is possible.

Route measures can be updated using the shortest path distance between the calibration points or using the existing measure distance between the points. In most applications, using the shortest path distance between the calibration points will be sufficient. Calibrating by measure distance should be used on data for which the length-to-measure ratio is not consistent at various locations along the input routes.

When calibrating using the shortest path distance, you can choose whether the output routes will have continuous measures when there are disjointed parts.

A search radius can be specified to limit how far a calibration point can be from a route. Points outside the search radius will not be used by the calibration process.

1. Click the Show/Hide ArcToolbox button on the Standard toolbar to show ArcToolbox.

2. Expand the Linear Referencing Tools.

3. Double-click the Calibrate Routes tool.

4. Type the Input Route Features filename and path or click the Browse button to select it.

5. Click the Route Identifier Field dropdown arrow and click the route identifier field.

6. Type the Input Point Features filename and path or click the Browse button to select it.

7. Click the Point Identifier Field dropdown arrow and click the point identifier field.

8. Click the Measure Field dropdown arrow and click the measure field.

9. Type the Output Route Feature Class filename and path or click the Browse button to specify the output location.

10. Optionally, click the Measure Calculation Method dropdown arrow and click a measure calculation method. ►

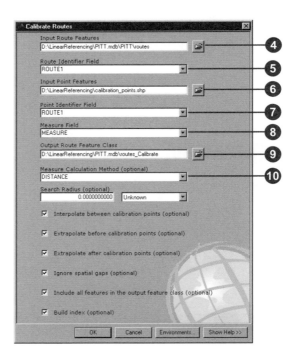

Tip

Calibrate Routes Wizard

The Calibrate Routes Wizard is available in ArcCatalog via the Customize dialog box. You can add it to your context window or toolbars.

See Also

For more information on adding a command to a context menu, see Using ArcCatalog.

See Also

For information on the optional parameters, click Show Help on the tool's dialog box.

11. Optionally, type the Search Radius that will be used to match the points to the routes and click the drop-down arrow to select the unit of measurement.

12. Click Environments. ▶

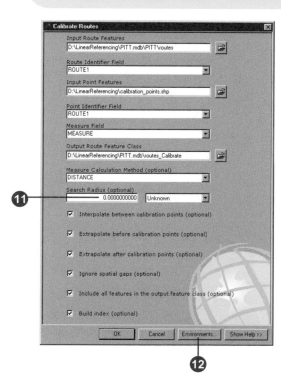

13. Expand Geodatabase Settings.

14. Click the Output M Domain dropdown arrow and click As Specified Below.

15. Type a value for Min M and Precision.

16. Click OK to close each dialog box.

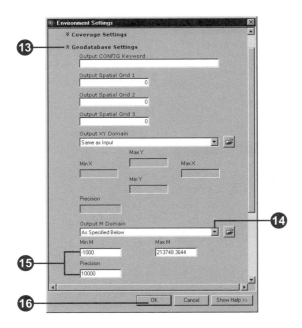

Migrating route data to a geodatabase

The Feature Class to Feature Class and Feature Class to Geodatabase scripts in ArcToolbox allow you to migrate route data from any supported format into a geodatabase. During the conversion, all measure values are preserved. The example in this section converts a coverage route system to a geodatabase feature class.

When migrating to a geodatabase, you can create a standalone feature class or a feature class in an existing dataset.

When creating or importing a feature class or feature dataset, you can specifiy the coordinate system, spatial domain, and precision in the environment settings. Set the spatial domain and precision carefully since once you've created the feature class the attributes cannot be changed.

If you're creating a feature class in an existing feature dataset, the new feature class will automatically take on the same coordinate system, spatial domain, and precision as the feature dataset, so there is no ▶

Migrating a coverage route system to a geodatabase

1. Right-click the coverage route system in the Catalog tree that you want to migrate, point to Export, then click To Geodatabase (single).

   Alternatively, access the Feature Class to Feature Class tool directly in the ArcToolbox Conversion Tools, To Geodatabase toolset.

2. Type the value of the Output Workspace parameter, or click the Browse button to choose this value.

   NOTE: The Output Workspace must already exist.

3. Type the value of the New Feature Class Name parameter.

4. Optionally, type a value for the Expression parameter, or click the Expression button and use the Query Builder to build the value for the parameter.

5. Optionally, edit the Field Info.

   Click a value in the NewFieldName field to change the field name.

   Click a value in the Visible field and click TRUE or FALSE to carry this field into the new feature class. ▶

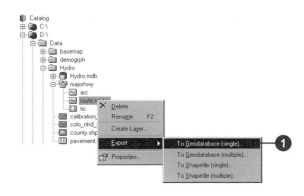

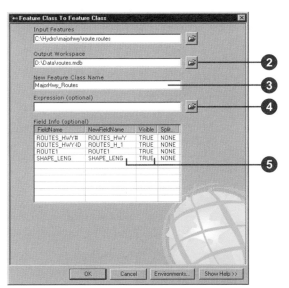

need to specify the spatial reference parameters in the Environment Settings before you import. The exception is the m domain, which you should always set when migrating data to a geodatabase. For more information about spatial references, see *Building a Geodatabase*.

You can optionally specify which fields to import and how to name them. You can also limit which features are imported by specifying an expression or a field list.

6. Click Environments.

7. Expand General Settings.

8. Click the Output has M Values dropdown arrow and click Same As Input.

9. Expand Geodatabase Settings.

10. Click the Output M Domain dropdown arrow and click As Specified Below.

11. Type a value for Min M and Precision.

12. Click OK to close each dialog box.

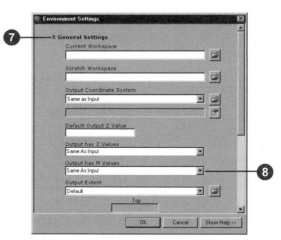

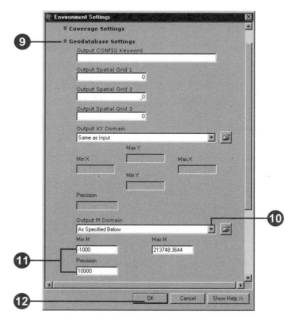

Displaying and querying routes and events 5

Geographic data is represented on a map as a *layer*. Route and event data aren't any different. ArcMap provides you with the tools to add route and event data to a map as a layer. ArcMap also provides you with many tools for symbolizing and labeling route and event layers in a wide variety of ways.

Once your route and event data have been added to a map, you can gain much insight by just looking at it. You may, however, want to discover spatial relationships that are not apparent to the naked eye. ArcMap provides you with a number of tools to find answers to questions such as Where is...? What is...? Where is the closest...? What's inside...? and What intersects...? In addition to these tools, ArcMap provides you with tools designed specifically for linear referencing data. With these additional tools, you can:

- Find route and measure information by pointing at your map.

- Find route locations on a map by providing route and measure information.

For more information on displaying and querying your data, refer to *Using ArcMap*.

The route identifier field

When route data is added to ArcMap, additional layer properties are exposed for working with this layer. One of these new properties is the route identifier field.

The *route identifier* uniquely identifies each route within a feature class. The route identifier field can be any numeric or character field in your route feature class.

Setting the route identifier field saves steps when using many of the linear referencing and dynamic segmentation dialog boxes and wizards in ArcMap.

Tip

Saving the route identifier field

If the layer is saved as a layer file (.lyr), the route identifier field is saved as well.

Setting the route identifier field

1. Right-click the route layer in the table of contents and click Properties.

2. Click the Routes tab.

3. Click the Route Identifier dropdown arrow and click the field that is to be used as the route identifier.

4. Click OK.

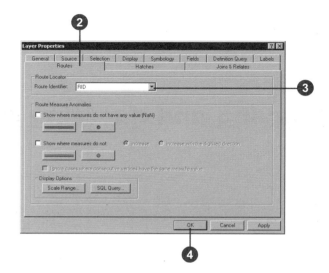

Querying route data

A lot of information can be derived from a map by just looking at it. There are times, however, when you need to know more. Because of this, ArcMap provides you with the tools for querying your maps in a wide variety of ways. In addition to the standard suite of map query tools, you can also find and identify route locations.

See Also

For more information on querying maps or adding commands to a toolbar or menu, see Using ArcMap.

Adding the Identify Route Locations tool

1. Click the Tools menu and click Customize.

2. Click the Commands tab.

3. Click Linear Referencing in the Categories list.

4. Drag the Identify Route Locations tool to the toolbar of your choice—for example, the Tools toolbar.

5. Click Close.

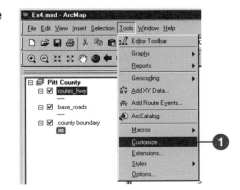

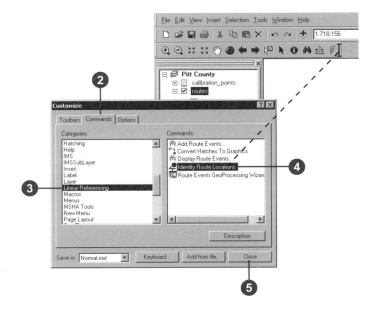

Tip

The Identify Route Locations tool is not enabled

The Identify Route Locations tool will not be enabled when there are no route layers in the map.

Tip

Route Identifier field

The values displayed on the branches of the route locations tree correspond to the values in the Route Identifier field. See 'Setting the route identifier field' in this chapter.

Tip

Layer dropdown list

Use the Layer dropdown list to identify route locations from specific layers only.

Identifying route locations

1. Click the Identify Route Locations tool.

2. Click the location on the route where you want route measure information.

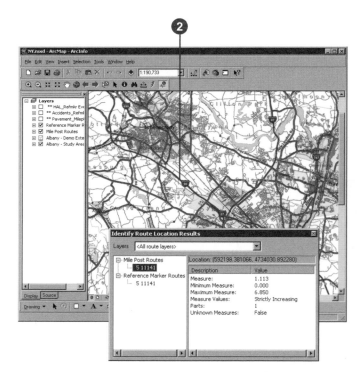

Controlling the text of the route location

When a route location is labeled, the text comes from two sources. The route identifier reflects the name of the layer's route identifier field. The measure reflects the description that is displayed on the right panel of the Identify Route Locations dialog box.

Changing what information is displayed

Right-click anywhere on the right panel of the Identify Route Locations dialog box to expose a context menu that allows you to control which route location information is displayed.

When you draw or label a route location, ArcMap default symbol properties are used. For more information on ArcMap default symbol properties, see Using ArcMap.

Labeling an identified route location with a text graphic

1. Right-click on a found route location and click Label route location.

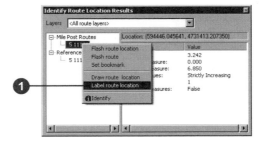

Route identifier field

The Find dialog box pays attention to the route identifier field. If you have not set the route identifier field, then you will need to click the Route Identifier dropdown arrow and click the field to be used for the route identifier between steps 3 and 4. See 'Setting the route identifier field' in this chapter.

Finding a route location

1. Click the Find tool on the ArcMap Tools toolbar.

2. Click the Route Locations tab.

3. Click the Route Reference dropdown arrow and click the layer that is the route reference.

4. Optionally, click the Load Routes button.

5. Click the Route dropdown arrow and click the route.

   Alternatively, type the route identifier in the Route dropdown list.

6. Click whether the route location will be point or line.

7. Type the route location information.

8. Click Find.

9. Right-click the found route location and explore the context choices available to you.

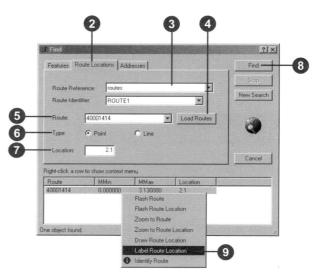

Hatching

Hatching is a type of labeling that is designed to post and label hatch marks or symbols at a regular interval along measured linear features. Hatching can be used for both distance-based and nondistance-based measures. Distance-based measures include kilometers, miles, feet, and meters. Nondistance-based measures include seismic shotpoint numbers where measure values generally increase in even intervals based on some nominal distance.

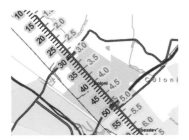 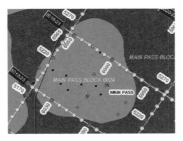

Hatching can be used in applications with either distance-based or nondistance-based measures.

Hatching concepts

To display hatches on a layer, you must define one or more *hatch classes* for the features you wish to hatch. Each hatch class is composed of one or more hatch definitions.

The easiest way to understand hatch classes and hatch definitions is to use a ruler analogy. On a ruler, there is a series of vertical lines, or hatches, separated by a regular interval. For example, on a centimeter (cm) ruler, the hatches are typically spaced every millimeter (mm). One millimeter is 1/10 of a centimeter, so the hatch interval is 0.1.

Not all the hatches on a ruler are the same. Some are longer than others. Further, some have text, while others do not. On a centimeter ruler, the hatches placed at every millimeter (0.1 cm) are the shortest. The hatches placed at every 5 millimeters (0.5 cm)

are a bit longer. The hatches placed every 10 millimeters (1 cm) are the longest. The longest hatches typically have text to indicate the measure value.

In this example, the ruler is a hatch class. It is a container for the hatch definitions. There are three hatch definitions. Each definition is placed at a multiple of the hatch interval. The longest hatches are placed at every 0.1 x 10 measure units. The second longest hatches are placed at every 0.1 x 5 measure units. The shortest hatches are placed at every 0.1 x 1 measure units.

```
 0 cm     1     2     3     4     5     6
|ıιιιιιıιιιıιιιιıιιιıιιιıιιιıιιιıιιιıιιιıιιιıιιιıιιıιι
```

In this example, the ruler represents a hatch class. The interval of the hatches is 0.1 cm (1 mm). There are three hatch definitions. Each definition is placed at a multiple of the hatch interval—10, 5, and 1, respectively. Some hatch definitions are labeled, while others are not.

When placed on a map, hatch definitions within a single hatch class will not draw on top of one another.

There is a special type of hatch definition known as an *end hatch definition*. An end hatch definition pays no attention to the specified hatch interval. Rather, it simply draws hatch marks at the low and high measure of a linear feature. For cases in which hatches get placed too close together near the end of a feature, it is possible to specify an end hatch tolerance, which prevents certain hatches from drawing if they are within the tolerance (specified in measure units) of an end hatch.

Imagine that you have linear features whose measures are in miles. You want to place a hatch every quarter of a mile. This is a hatch interval of 0.25. Further, you want the hatches placed at every 0.25, 0.5, and 1 mile to look different (different length, different color). You want the hatches every mile to have text. Last, you want hatches at the ends of the feature. These end hatches are to look different from all other hatches and will have text. The following example demonstrates conceptually how hatching works in this scenario.

How hatching works

In this example, the line is 4.0 miles long, and the hatch interval is 0.25. To make hatches look like the following, four hatch definitions are necessary.

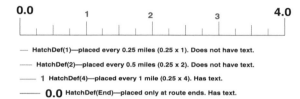

— HatchDef(1)—placed every 0.25 miles (0.25 x 1). Does not have text.

— HatchDef(2)—placed every 0.5 miles (0.25 x 2). Does not have text.

— 1 HatchDef(4)—placed every 1 mile (0.25 x 4). Has text.

— 0.0 HatchDef(End)—placed only at route ends. Has text.

Step 1: The hatch definition with the highest multiple of the hatch interval—HatchDef(4)—is placed first. Because an end hatch definition has been specified, no hatches are placed at the ends even though the measure values are divisible by the hatch interval.

Step 2: The hatch definition with the next highest multiple of the hatch interval—HatchDef(2)—is placed. These hatches will not overwrite hatches that have already been placed.

Step 3: The hatch definition with the next highest multiple of the hatch interval—HatchDef(1)—is placed. These hatches will not overwrite hatches that have already been placed.

Step 4: The end hatch definition—HatchDef(End)—will be placed.

Hatching options

There are many ways in which you can control how hatches appear on a map. The following illustrate some of the ways hatches can be manipulated.

All of the hatch definitions in a hatch class can be offset by the same amount. Alternately, each individual hatch definition can have its own offset.

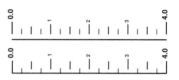

Each hatch definition can be displayed to the left of, centered on, or to the right of a feature. When set to center, hatches will be labeled to the left of the feature.

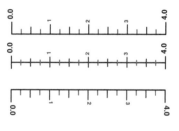

Hatching can start at a measure location other than the low measure. Further, hatching can finish at a location other than the high measure.

In the case in which a feature's geometry has multiple parts, it is possible to apply hatches to the feature as a whole or to each part individually.

By default, the placement of
hatches is adjusted to the
hatch interval. This means
that in cases in which a line's
low measure is not divisible
by the interval, the first
hatch will be placed at the

first measure value that is divisible by the hatch interval. For
example, a line whose measures range from 1.1 to 5.2 will have its
first hatch placed at 1.25 when the hatch interval is 0.25. This
behavior can be turned off. Note that end hatch definitions are
not affected by this setting and are not shown in this example.

In cases in which a feature's
high measure is not divisible
by the hatch interval and an
end hatch definition has
been defined, it is possible to

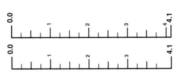

get two hatches that are very close to or on top of one another.
To avoid this, it is possible to specify an end hatch tolerance,
which informs the hatching algorithm to not place hatches when
they fall within the tolerance of the end hatch. The end hatch
tolerance is specified in route measure units, and its value is
typically set to a value that is less than the hatch interval.

Hatches are drawn perpendicular to the feature. It is possible to
specify a supplemental angle
that is added to the
calculated angle.

Hatch text is flipped as the
direction of the feature
changes. This is to make
the text more readable. This
can be turned off so the
text is always oriented in
the direction of increasing
measure.

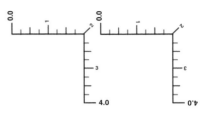

Hatches can also be placed
only at the route ends. In this
case, it is not necessary to
specify a hatch interval.

Creating and managing hatches

Hatches are a feature layer property. As such, hatches are created
and managed on the Layer Properties dialog box.

The Hatches tab on the Layer Properties dialog box has three
views: the Hatch Class view, the Hatch Definition view, and the
End Hatch Definition view. The hatch class view is enabled when
a hatch class is selected in the hatch tree. The hatch definition
view is enabled when a hatch definition is selected in the hatch
tree. The end hatch definition view is enabled when an end hatch
definition is selected in the hatch tree.

Hatch Class view

Note that a hatch class is highlighted in the hatch tree.

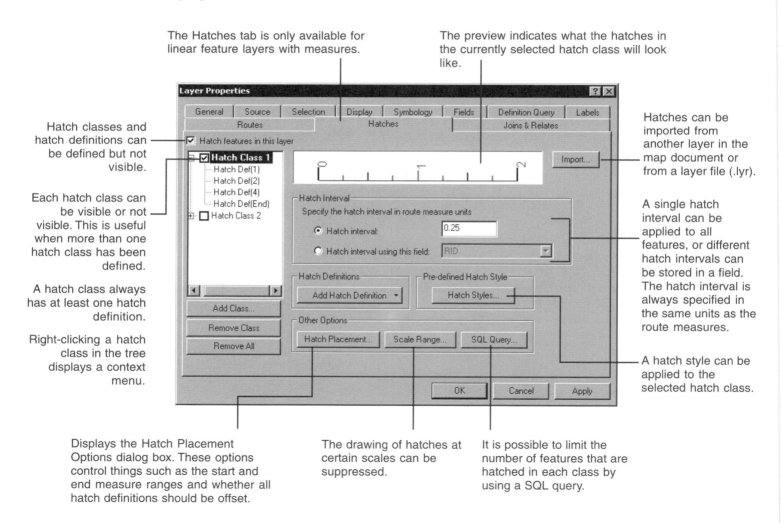

The Hatches tab is only available for linear feature layers with measures.

The preview indicates what the hatches in the currently selected hatch class will look like.

Hatch classes and hatch definitions can be defined but not visible.

Each hatch class can be visible or not visible. This is useful when more than one hatch class has been defined.

A hatch class always has at least one hatch definition.

Right-clicking a hatch class in the tree displays a context menu.

Hatches can be imported from another layer in the map document or from a layer file (.lyr).

A single hatch interval can be applied to all features, or different hatch intervals can be stored in a field. The hatch interval is always specified in the same units as the route measures.

A hatch style can be applied to the selected hatch class.

Displays the Hatch Placement Options dialog box. These options control things such as the start and end measure ranges and whether all hatch definitions should be offset.

The drawing of hatches at certain scales can be suppressed.

It is possible to limit the number of features that are hatched in each class by using a SQL query.

Hatch Definition view

Note that a hatch definition is highlighted in the hatch tree.

The selected hatch definition is highlighted using the ArcMap selection color.

A hatch definition is placed at a multiple of the hatch interval. The hatch interval is set on the Hatch Class view.

A hatch definition's name includes the multiple of the hatch interval at which the hatches are to be placed.

No two definitions within the same class can have the same multiple of the hatch interval.

Right-clicking a hatch definition in the tree displays a context menu.

A hatch definition can be symbolized with either a line or marker symbol.

The line length and lateral offset properties are specified in the units that are set on the Hatch Placement Options dialog box.

Displays the Hatch Orientation dialog box.

Displays the Label Settings dialog box.

Each hatch definition can be labeled with the route measure.

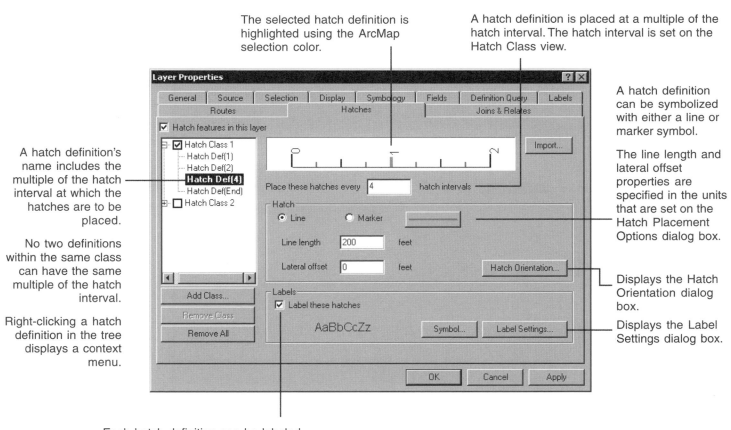

End Hatch Definition view

Note that an end hatch definition is highlighted in the hatch tree.

The selected end hatch definition is highlighted using ArcMap selection color.

An end hatch definition is a special type of hatch definition. These hatches are only placed at the line ends.

Right-clicking an end hatch definition in the tree displays a context menu.

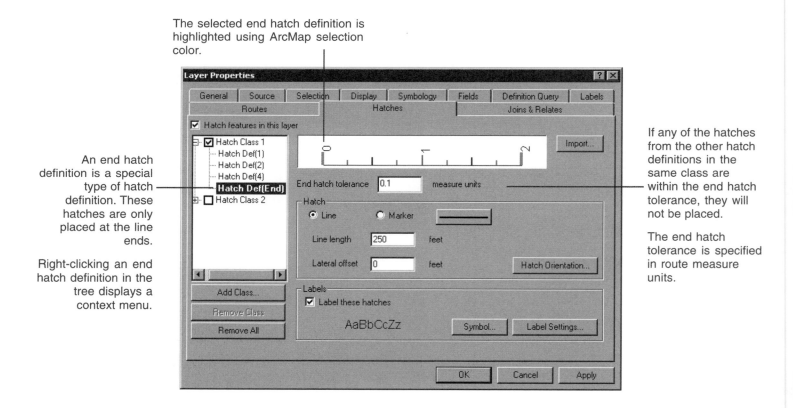

If any of the hatches from the other hatch definitions in the same class are within the end hatch tolerance, they will not be placed.

The end hatch tolerance is specified in route measure units.

Hatch Placement Options dialog box

This dialog box is initiated by clicking the Hatch Placement button on the Hatch Class view. The settings made on this dialog box apply to all the hatch definitions that make up the selected hatch class.

The distance units apply to offsets and hatch definition lengths. They do not refer in any way to the hatch interval, which is specified in route measure units.

The default distance units are the same as the active data frame's display units.

It is possible to start hatching at a value other than the lowest measure. A single value can be applied to all features, or different values can be stored in a field. These values are always specified in route measure units.

In some cases, the low measure of a line is not exactly divisible by the hatch interval. The first hatch placed will be adjusted to a measure value that is divisible by the hatch interval. This behavior can be turned off.

All hatch definitions in a class can be offset by a value. A single offset can be applied to all features, or different offsets can be stored in a field.

Note that it is possible to offset individual hatch definitions. This is done on the Hatch Definition view.

It is possible to finish hatching at a value other than the highest measure. A single value can be applied to all features, or different values can be stored in a field. These values are always specified in route measure units.

In some cases, a line might have multiple parts. It is possible to apply all hatch settings to each part individually.

Hatch Placement Options

Distance Units: Feet

☐ Offset hatch definitions   (feet)
  ⦿ Offset hatches: 0
  ○ Offset hatches using this field: RID

☐ Start hatching at a value other than the lowest measure
  ⦿ Start hatching at: 0
  ○ Start hatching using this field: RID

☐ Finish hatching at a value other than the highest measure
  ⦿ Finish hatching at: 0
  ○ Finish hatching using this field: RID

☑ Adjust hatch placement to hatch interval
☐ Apply hatch settings to each part

OK   Cancel

Hatch Orientation dialog box

This dialog box is initiated by clicking the Hatch Orientation button on the Hatch Definition view. The settings made on this dialog box apply only to the currently selected hatch definition.

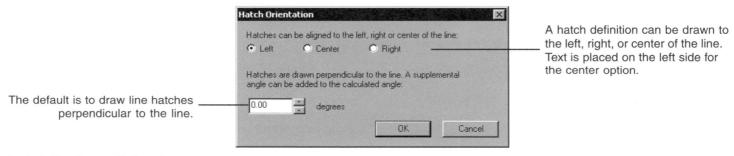

The default is to draw line hatches perpendicular to the line.

A hatch definition can be drawn to the left, right, or center of the line. Text is placed on the left side for the center option.

Label Settings dialog box

This dialog box is initiated by clicking the Label Settings button on the Hatch Definition view. The settings made on this dialog box apply only to the currently selected hatch definition.

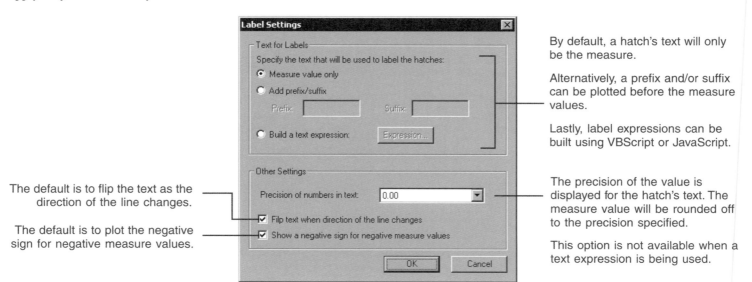

By default, a hatch's text will only be the measure.

Alternatively, a prefix and/or suffix can be plotted before the measure values.

Lastly, label expressions can be built using VBScript or JavaScript.

The default is to flip the text as the direction of the line changes.

The default is to plot the negative sign for negative measure values.

The precision of the value is displayed for the hatch's text. The measure value will be rounded off to the precision specified.

This option is not available when a text expression is being used.

Displaying hatches

Hatches are line or marker symbols displayed on top of features at an interval specified in route measure units. Hatches allow you to make maps that are suitable for almost any application that uses measured linear features.

Layers based on linear features with measures always have at least one hatch class associated with them. Initially, the default hatch class contains one hatch definition. Additional hatch definitions can be added to this hatch class. Each hatch definition has its own set of properties. These include the multiple of the hatch interval at which the hatches in the hatch definition will be placed, the line or marker symbol of the hatches, and whether the hatches will be labeled. The use of multiple hatch definitions allows you to design complex hatching schemes.

Because hatch definitions might share many of the same properties, it is possible to copy the properties of a hatch definition and change only the properties that are different.

Any number of hatch classes can be associated with a layer. ▶

Hatching features in a layer

1. Right-click the layer in the table of contents that you want to hatch and click Properties.

2. Click the Hatches tab.

3. Check Hatch features in this layer.

4. Type an appropriate Hatch interval.

5. Click Hatch Def(1).

   The Hatch Definition view becomes active.

6. Type an appropriate Line length. ▶

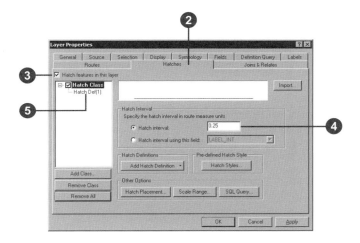

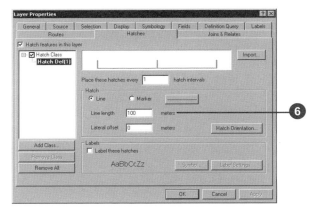

Each hatch class can contain any number of hatch definitions. One reason to create multiple hatch classes is to hatch some features one way and other features another way. To do this, you would associate a SQL query with your hatch classes. Another reason to have multiple classes is to have hatches appear differently at different scales. To do this, you would specify a scale range with your hatch classes.

In situations when you need hatches at the end of features, you need to add an end hatch definition to the hatch class.

To appear on a map, hatches must be turned on via a check box. Note that it is possible to turn each individual class on or off as well.

To save time, it is possible to import hatches from another layer. These layers may be in the map or may have been stored on disk as a layer file (.lyr). Note that if any of the hatch properties in the layer you are trying to import from are based on a field—for example, the hatch interval— then that field must exist in the layer you are trying to import to.

Another time-saving method is the use of hatch styles. For more information on hatch ▶

7. Right-click the hatch class and click Add Hatch Definition.

   The Hatch Definition view becomes active.

8. Type an appropriate multiple of the hatch interval.

9. Type an appropriate Line length.

10. Check Label these hatches. ▶

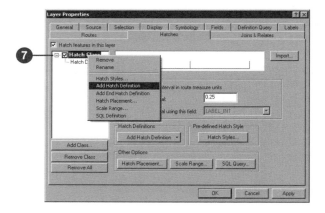

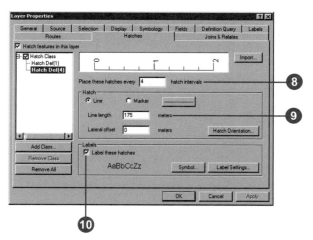

styles, see 'Hatch styles' in this chapter.

Hatches do not respect the ArcMap overposting environment. As such, hatches and their labels can overlap one another. To avoid this, specifying a different hatch interval often alleviates the problem. In some situations, however, it is desirable to convert hatches to graphics so they can be moved on the map.

Hatches do not appear on the map

If hatches do not appear after you have set up your hatch classes and hatch definitions, make sure that (1) the Hatch features in this layer box is checked, (2) the box beside each hatch class in the tree is checked, (3) the specified hatch interval is appropriate for the data, and (4) all hatch definitions that use a line symbol have an appropriate line length specified.

Stopping the drawing process

If you selected a hatch interval that is too small, too many hatches will be drawn on the screen. The drawing process can be stopped by pressing the Esc key.

11. Right-click the hatch class and click Add End Hatch Definition.

    The End Hatch Definition view becomes active.

12. Type an appropriate End hatch tolerance if necessary.

13. Type an appropriate Line length.

14. Check Label these hatches.

15. Click OK.

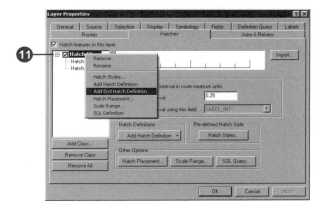

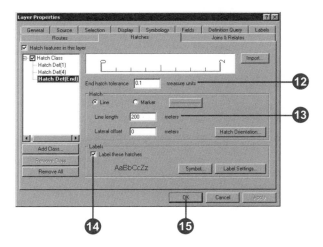

Making hatches and their labels bigger when you zoom in

As you zoom in and out on your map, the sizes of the hatches and their labels do not change. If you want the hatches and text to scale with the map, set a reference scale. Right-click the data frame and click Set Reference Scale.

Importing hatches from another layer

1. Right-click the layer in the table of contents that you want to hatch and click Properties.

2. Click the Hatches tab.

3. Click Import.

4. Click the Layer dropdown arrow and click the layer you want to import hatches from.

   Alternately, click the Browse button and navigate to the layer file (.lyr) that you want to import hatches from.

5. Click OK on the Import Hatches dialog box.

6. Click OK.

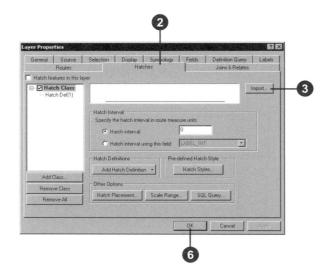

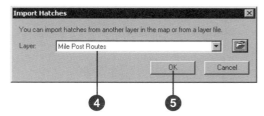

Copying a hatch definition's properties

1. Right-click the hatch definition that you want to define the properties for and click Copy Properties From.

2. Click the hatch definition dropdown arrow and click the hatch definition whose properties you want to copy.

3. Click OK.

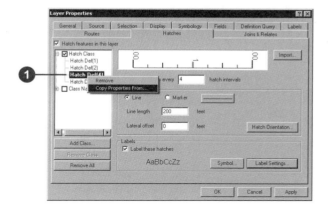

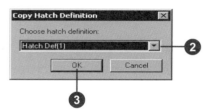

Adding the Convert Hatches to Graphics command

1. Click the Tools menu and click Customize.

2. Click the Toolbars tab.

3. Check Context Menus in the Toolbars list.

   The Context Menus toolbar appears. ▶

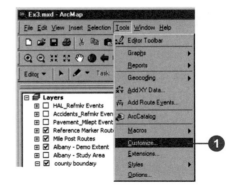

See Also

For more information on adding commands to a toolbar or menu, see Using ArcMap.

4. Click the Context Menus dropdown list and click Feature Layer Context Menu.

5. Click the Commands tab.

6. Click Linear Referencing in the Categories list.

7. Click the Save in dropdown arrow and click where you want your customization saved.

8. Drag the Convert Hatches To Graphics command to the Feature Layer Context Menu.

9. Click Close.

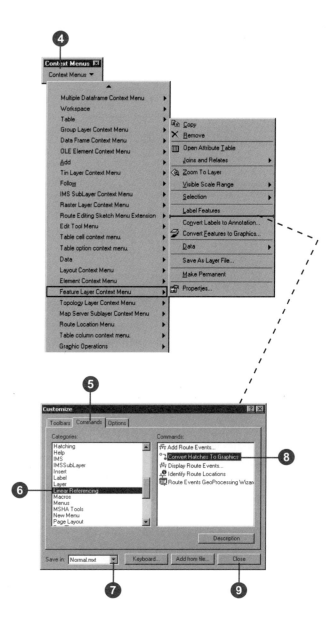

Converting hatches to graphics

1. Right-click the layer in the table of contents whose hatches you want to convert to graphics and click Convert Hatches to Graphics.

2. Click the features for which you want to create graphics.

3. Uncheck any hatch classes you do not want converted to graphics if appropriate.

4. Click the Target annotation group dropdown arrow and click the annotation target where you want to add the graphics.

   Alternately, type the name of a new target annotation group.

5. Click OK.

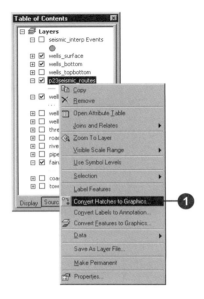

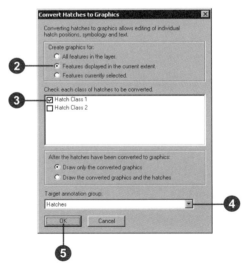

Manipulating the text on hatches

Every hatch definition may or may not be labeled. When labeled, you have control over things such as the text symbol that is used and whether or not the text will automatically be flipped as the direction of the route changes.

By default, the text associated with a hatch is the route measure at the hatch location. This text can be supplemented with a prefix and/or suffix value.

For more advanced needs, you can programmatically generate a hatch's text by writing a script in Microsoft® VBScript™ or JavaScript™. Your script can include any valid statements those programming languages support.

When writing a script, you access the route measure for each hatch using the *esri__measure* constant value.

The script used in the following example tells the hatching algorithm not to label a hatch if its measure value is within 0.1 measure units of the value stored in a field named MMAX. This method can be used instead of an end hatch tolerance, which tells the hatch algorithm not to draw either the hatch or its label.

Generating the text on hatches using a script

1. Right-click the layer in the table of contents that you want to hatch and click Properties.

2. Click the Hatches tab.

3. Follow steps 3 through 14 of 'Hatching features in a layer' if necessary.

4. Click the hatch definition of your choice.

5. Make sure the Label these hatches check box is checked.

6. Click Label Settings.

7. Click Build a text expression.

8. Click Expression. ▶

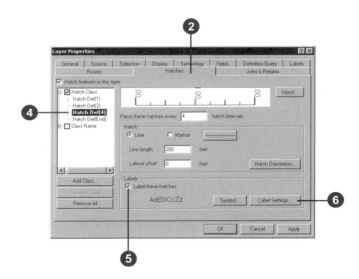

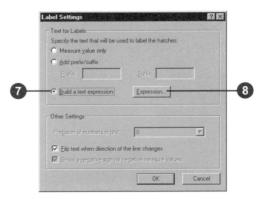

See Also

For more information on VBScript and/or JavaScript, click the Help button on the Hatch Text Expression dialog box.

9. Check Advanced.

10. Type a VBScript or JavaScript expression.

    ArcMap automatically creates a FindLabel function in your code. FindLabel should evaluate to a string.

11. Click Verify to make sure there are no syntax errors.

12. Click OK on the Hatch Text Expression dialog box.

13. Click OK on the Label Settings dialog box.

14. Click OK.

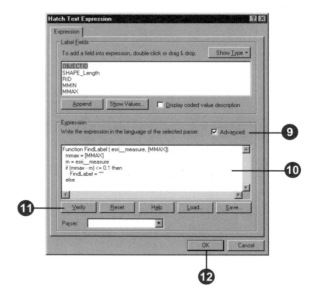

```
Function FindLabel (esri__measure, [MMAX])
  mmax = [MMAX]
  m = esri__measure
  if (mmax - m) <= 0.1 then
      FindLabel = ""
  else
    FindLabel = cstr(round(m,2))
  end if
End Function
```

Hatch styles

A *hatch style* stores the symbols and the settings of the hatch definitions that make up a hatch class. Hatch styles help you maintain standards for displaying your hatches on multiple maps with multiple data sources.

When setting up hatch styles, it is important to note that some of the properties available when setting up a hatch class are not available when setting up a hatch style. These are the properties that are based on attributes, such as class level offsets, start measures, and finish measures.

Like any other style in ArcMap, hatch styles are stored in a style file (.style). Unlike other styles, however, there are no industry-standard hatch styles that come with ArcMap. It is up to you to create your own hatch styles.

Whether you are creating a new hatch style from scratch or altering the properties of an existing one, you use the Style Manager dialog box to work with hatch styles.

See Also

For more information on styles, see Using ArcMap.

Creating a new hatch style in the Style Manager

1. Click the Tools menu, point to Styles, then click Style Manager.

2. Click the Hatches folder in the style tree in the ESRI style file (.style) in which you want to create a new hatch style.

3. Right-click in the open space in the Style contents window, point to New, then click Hatch.

4. Set the style's properties on the Hatch Style properties dialog box and click OK.

5. Name the new hatch style.

6. Click close to close the Style Manager dialog box.

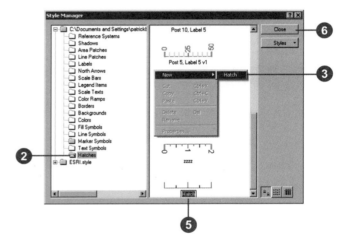

Saving a hatch class as a hatch style

1. Click the hatch class that you want to save as a hatch style.

2. Click Hatch Styles.

3. Click Save.

4. Type the name of the new hatch style.

5. Click OK.

6. Click OK on the Hatch Style dialog box.

7. Click Apply.

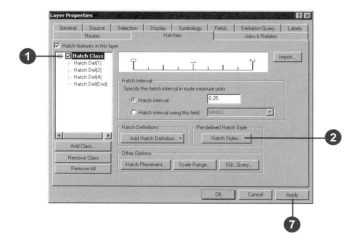

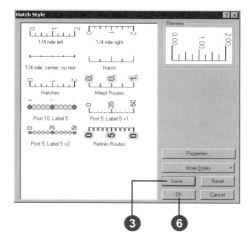

Tip

Applying a hatch style

If you apply a hatch style to a hatch class that already has some hatch definitions in addition to the default definition, they will be overwritten by the hatch definitions in the hatch style.

Applying a hatch style to a hatch class

1. Click the hatch class to which you want to apply a hatch style.

2. Click Hatch Styles.

3. Click the hatch style you want to use.

4. Click OK.

5. Click Apply.

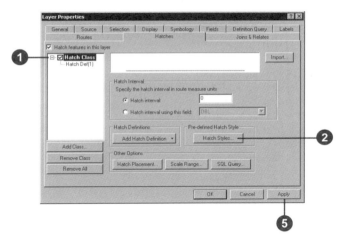

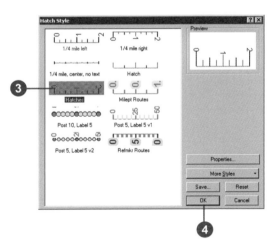

Route measure anomalies

The ArcGIS system does not place any constraints on route measures. Route measures can always increase with respect to a route's digitized direction, always decrease with respect to a route's digitized direction, or be some combination of increasing and decreasing values. Lastly, route measures may be unknown (NaN).

Route measure anomalies are portions of routes where the measures do not conform to the standards your application expects. With the ability to display what you deem to be route measure anomalies in ArcMap, you can ensure that the measures on your routes conform to the needs of your application. Seeing where route measure anomalies occur can help you isolate routes that may need to have their measures edited.

Tip

Scale ranges and SQL queries
Use a scale range and/or a SQL query to control how route measure anomalies are displayed.

Displaying route measure anomalies

1. Right-click the route layer in the table of contents and click Properties.

2. Click the Routes tab.

3. Click the Route Measure Anomalies you want to display and change the symbology as necessary.

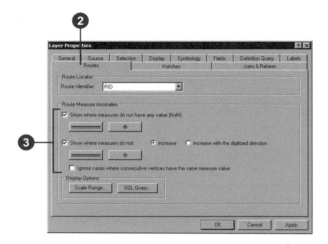

Dynamic segmentation

Geographic data is represented on a map as a layer. Route events are no different. To display route events on a map, however, you must first define the parameters of the relationship between the table storing the events and the routes that the events reference.

Dynamic segmentation (DynSeg) is the process of computing the map location (shape) of events stored in an event table. Dynamic segmentation is what allows multiple sets of attributes to be associated with any portion of a linear feature.

The result of the dynamic segmentation process is a dynamic feature class known as a route event source. A route event source can serve as the data source of a feature layer in ArcMap.

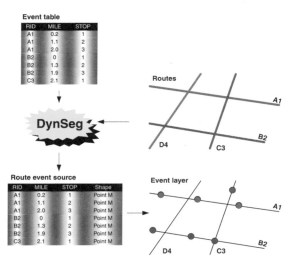

The result of the dynamic segmentation process can be displayed on a map as a layer.

For the most part, a dynamic feature layer behaves like any other feature layer. It is possible to decide whether or not to display it, the scale at which it should be visible, what features or subset of features to display, how to draw the features, whether to store it as a layer file (.lyr), whether to export it, and so on.

A route event source can be edited in ArcMap. It is important to note, however, that it is possible to only edit the attributes. The shapes of a route event source, however, cannot be edited because they are generated by the dynamic segmentation process. When you edit a route event, you are actually editing the underlying event table. As such, there may be some editing limitations imposed by the event table. For example, it is not possible to directly edit the attributes of a route event source created from a delimited text file table since ArcMap does not allow text files to be edited directly.

Advanced dynamic segmentation options

Point events as multipoint features

When a point event is located along a route, a point feature is created. In some applications, however, route measures are not unique. For these applications, it might be desirable to have point events treated as multipoint features.

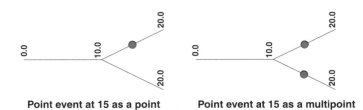

Point event at 15 as a point   **Point event at 15 as a multipoint**

Point events can be located along routes as point features or multipoint features.

Event locating angles

When a point event is located along a route, it is often desirable to know the angle of the route where the event is placed. For example, you might need to rotate the marker symbol that is used to display the event so it is oriented to the route and not the map. Further, you might need to rotate a point event's label.

The dynamic segmentation process can calculate either the normal (perpendicular) or tangent angle. Further, it is possible to calculate the complement of these angles so you can, for example, control the side of the route on which a rotated label appears.

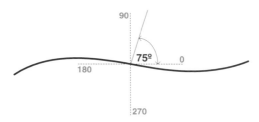

The dynamic segmentation process can calculate the angle of a route at a point event's location.

Event locating errors

The dynamic segmentation process creates a shape for each row in the input route event table. In some cases, however, the shape of the event feature might be empty. This happens when there was some reason that the event could not be properly located. In other cases, an event can only be partially located; this happens for line events only.

The dynamic segmentation process can expose the locating error, if any, for each event in an event table as a field. This field is useful when performing quality assurance tests on your event tables.

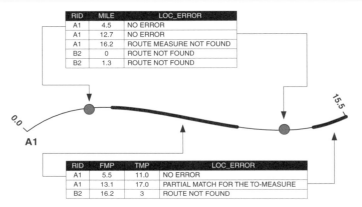

RID	MILE	LOC_ERROR
A1	4.5	NO ERROR
A1	12.7	NO ERROR
A1	16.2	ROUTE MEASURE NOT FOUND
B2	0	ROUTE NOT FOUND
B2	1.3	ROUTE NOT FOUND

RID	FMP	TMP	LOC_ERROR
A1	5.5	11.0	NO ERROR
A1	13.1	17.0	PARTIAL MATCH FOR THE TO-MEASURE
B2	16.2	3	ROUTE NOT FOUND

The dynamic segmentation process is aware of the locating status of each event. This information can be exposed as a field.

Event offsets

In some applications, events with an offset are to be drawn to the right of the route. In other applications, events with an offset are to be drawn to the left. The dynamic segmentation process allows you to control which side of the route events with offsets is drawn.

Adding route events

A *route location* describes a portion of a route or a single location along a route. When route locations are stored in tables, they are known as *route event tables*. Route event tables are typically organized around a common theme. For example, an event table for highways might include speed limits, year of resurfacing, present condition, and accidents.

There are two types of route events: point and line. Point ▶

Tip

Route identifier field
The Add Route Events dialog box will pay attention to a route layer's route identifier field.

Tip

Attribute indexes
Dynamic segmentation performance is improved with the use of an attribute index on the route identifier field in both the event table and the route reference.

Tip

Displaying route events
Right-click an event table in the table of contents and click Display Route Events.

Adding route events from the ArcMap Tools menu

1. Click Tools and click Add Route Events.

2. Click the Route Reference dropdown arrow and click the route reference layer.

   Alternately, click the Browse button and navigate to the route reference feature class.

3. Click the Route Identifier dropdown arrow and click the route identifier field if necessary.

4. Click the Event Table dropdown arrow and click the event table.

   Alternately, click the Browse button and navigate to the event table.

5. Click the Route Identifier dropdown arrow and click the route identifier.

6. Click the type of events the route event table contains.

7. For point events, click the Measure dropdown arrow and click the Measure field.

   For line events, click the From-Measure dropdown arrow and click the from-measure field. Click the To-Measure dropdown arrow and click the to-measure field.

8. Optionally, click the Offset dropdown arrow and click the offset field. ▶

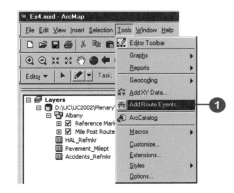

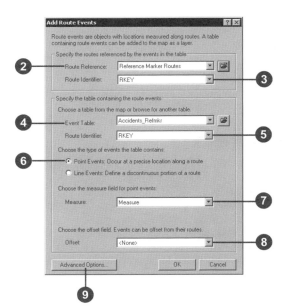

events occur at precise locations along a route. Line events describe a portion of a route.

A route event table has at least two fields: a route identifier and one or two measure locations. The route identifier indicates the route the event is located along. The measure location is either one or two values describing the positions on the route where the event occurs.

The process of computing the map location of events stored in an event table is known as dynamic segmentation.

The result of the dynamic segmentation process is a route event source, which can be used by a layer in a map. ▶

9. Click Advanced Options.

10. Click all of the advanced dynamic segmentations you want applied to the route event source.

11. Click OK on the Advanced Route Events dialog box.

12. Click OK.

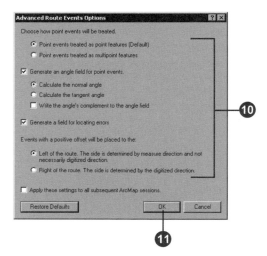

Tip

Advanced options

You can have the advanced dynamic segmentation options applied to subsequent ArcMap sessions by checking Apply these settings to all subsequent ArcMap sessions in the Advanced Route Events Options dialog box.

Tip

Layer files

If a layer based on route events is saved as a layer file (.lyr), the dynamic segmentation process will automatically be performed the next time you add the layer to your ArcMap document.

The Make Route Event Layer geoprocessing tool can be used in ArcCatalog or ArcMap. The result is an in-memory layer that can be used in other geoprocessing operations. Once created, this layer is available in the tool dropdown menus. If using ArcMap, the layer will appear in the table of contents.

For more information on in-memory layers see *Geoprocessing in ArcGIS.*

Tip

Add geoprocessing results to the display

In ArcMap, if you want the results of the Make Route Event Layer tool automatically added to your map's table of contents, check Add results of geoprocessing operations to the display, on the Geoprocessing tab of the Tools/Options dialog box.

Adding route events using ArcToolbox

1. Click the Show/Hide ArcToolbox button on the Standard menu to show ArcToolbox.

2. Expand the Linear Referencing Tools.

3. Double-click the Make Route Event Layer tool.

4. Click the Input Route Features dropdown arrow and click the route reference layer.

    Alternately, click the Browse button and navigate to the route reference feature class.

5. Click the Route Identifier Field dropdown arrow and click the route identifier field.

6. Click the Input Event Table dropdown arrow and click the event table.

    Alternately, click the Browse button and navigate to the event table.

7. Click the Route Identifier Field dropdown arrow and click the route identifier field. ▶

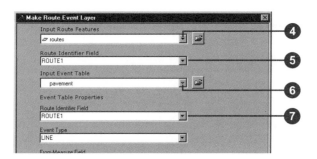

8. Click the Event Type dropdown arrow and click the type of event.

9. For point events, click the Measure dropdown arrow and click the Measure field.

    For line events, click the From-Measure dropdown arrow and click the from-measure field. Click the To-Measure dropdown arrow and click the to-measure field.

10. Type a Layer Name for this layer.

11. Optionally, click the Offset Field dropdown arrow and click the offset field.

12. Click OK.

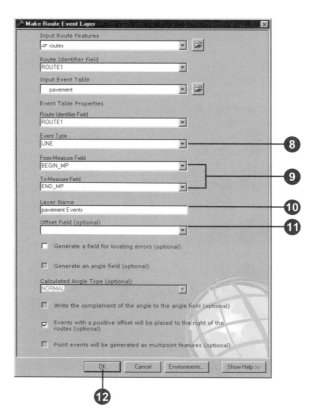

Editing routes

6

In addition to the display and query of routes and events, ArcMap is the application for creating and editing route features in your spatial database. ArcMap has tools for editing routes that are stored in shapefiles or geodatabase feature classes.

When editing routes, it is important to remember that you are simply editing linear features. If you already know how to edit linear features, you already know how to edit routes. The one thing that differentiates the editing of routes from other linear features is the presence of measure values stored with the feature's vertices. Hence, the editing of route features can be thought of as two distinct processes. The first is the editing of the route's geometry. The second is the editing of the route's measures.

This chapter shows you how to edit routes and route measures in ArcMap. Route editing requires prior knowledge of editing linear features in ArcMap. It is assumed that you already have a good understanding of how to edit linear features in ArcMap. For more information, see *Editing in ArcMap*.

ArcInfo and ArcEditor

Adding the Route Editing toolbar

Before you edit your route data in ArcMap, you need to add the Route Editing toolbar.

Tip

Adding the Editor toolbar
You should also ensure that the Editor toolbar has been added. To do this, click the Editor Toolbar button 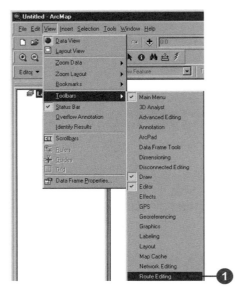 *on the ArcMap Standard toolbar.*

Tip

Adding the Route Editing toolbar using the Editor menu
From the Editor menu on the ArcMap Editor toolbar, point to More Editing Tools and click Route Editing.

Tip

Adding the Route Editing toolbar using the Customize dialog box
From the ArcMap Tools menu, click Customize, click the Toolbars tab, then click Route Editing.

1. In ArcMap, click the View menu, point to Toolbars, then click Route Editing.

2. Click the toolbar's title bar and drag it to the ArcMap application window.

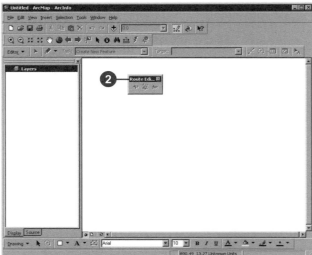

Creating routes from existing lines

ArcMap provides a variety of tools for creating linear features. Because a route is simply a linear feature with measures, if you are familiar with the various techniques for creating linear features, you are already familiar with some of the techniques for creating routes.

The following pages outline the steps for creating routes from existing line features. The number of steps differs depending on whether you want to create a simple or complex route. A complex route loops back on itself or branches.

When you create routes from existing lines, you must select the lines whose geometry you want to copy to create the route. The selected features can be from one or more of the linear feature layers already in your map. Further, they can be from any supported data format.

You can use any method available to you to select the linear features. For example, you can use the Edit tool on the Editor toolbar, the Select Features tool on the Tools toolbar, Select by Attributes, and so on. ▶

Creating a simple route

1. On the Editor toolbar, click Start Editing from the Editor menu.

2. Click the Task dropdown arrow and click Create New Feature.

3. Click the Target layer dropdown arrow and click a route layer.

4. Using any available method, select the linear feature or features whose geometry you want to copy to make the route.

   For example, click the Edit tool on the Editor toolbar, move the mouse pointer over a feature, and click the feature. Press the Shift key and continue to click all the features you want to use to create the route.

   The selected features will be highlighted.

5. Click the Make Route button on the Route Editing toolbar. ▶

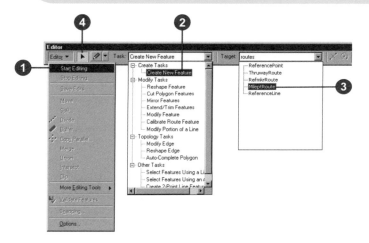

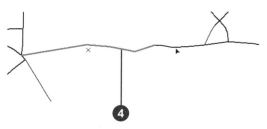

ArcInfo and ArcEditor

Once the linear features have been selected, you will use the Make Route dialog box to set the parameters for how your new route will be created.

The first parameter you set is the start point. This is where the route measure values will begin. There are two ways to set the start point. First, you can click a point on the map. When you choose this option, you will note that as you move your mouse around the map, the start point automatically snaps to one of the selected feature's endpoints. Second, you can use a coordinate priority of lower left, lower right, upper left, or upper right. These coordinate priorities are determined using the minimum bounding rectangle around the selected set of linear features. The endpoint from the selected features that is closest to the chosen coordinate priority will be where the measures start. ▶

Tip

Cannot see the start point on the map

If you cannot see the start point on the map, it may be because you are not zoomed out far enough to see all of the endpoints of the selected features. Note that you can interact with other ArcMap commands and tools (e.g., Pan, Zoom Out, Zoom to Selected Features) when the Make Route dialog box is displayed.

6. Click the Start Point button.

7. Move your mouse over the selected linear features and click the map when the start point is where you want the route measures to start.

8. Click the option for how you want the route measure values to be obtained.

9. Adjust the Multiply measures by and Start measure values if necessary.

10. Click Make Route.

    The newly created route is now selected.

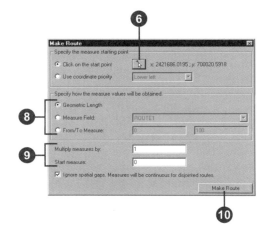

The next parameter you set indicates how the measure values are to be obtained. When you choose the geometric length option, it is important to realize that the geometric length of each selected feature is determined in the units of the target layer's coordinate system and not necessarily the feature's native coordinate system. This is to account for the fact that within a single data frame, features with different coordinate systems can be projected on the fly.

The measure field option is only enabled when all the selected linear features are from the same layer. Measure values on the new route will be accumulated using the values in this field.

Use the From/To option when you know the start and end measure values for the new route. All measure values between the start and end will be interpolated for you.

Multiplying measures is useful when you want to convert between measure units. For example, your route data is stored in a feature class with coordinate system units in feet. You want the measures on your routes to be in miles. You would multiply your measures by 0.0001893994 to convert from feet to miles. The measure multiplication factor is applied ►

Creating a complex (looping) route

1. Click the Task dropdown arrow and click Create New Feature.

2. Click the Target layer dropdown arrow and click a route layer.

3. Using any available method, select a simple chain of linear features that do not form a loop.

   For example, click the Edit tool on the Editor toolbar, move the mouse pointer over a feature, and click the feature. Press the Shift key and continue to click all the features you want to use to create the route.

   The selected features will be highlighted.

4. Click the Make Route button on the Route Editing toolbar. ►

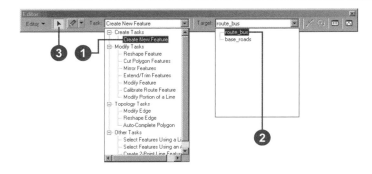

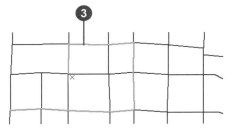

before the selected lines are merged to create a route.

The Start measure option is useful when you want your new route to have a start measure other than 0.

The last parameter you set indicates whether or not you want the measures to be continuous on disjointed routes. Note that if you choose to have noncontinuous measures, the gap distance is calculated using the units of the target layer's coordinate system. This might cause unexpected measure values, for example, when you use a field that stores mileage values to accumulate the measure and the target layer's coordinate system units are meters. Note that this check box is not available when the From/To option has been chosen to set the measures.

Once the new route has been created in the target feature ▶

Tip
Coordinates or measures out of bounds

If you get the Coordinates or measures out of bounds message when creating a route, it is because the measure values that are being applied to the new route do not fit in the m domain. For more information, see Chapter 4, 'Creating Route data'.

5. Click the Start Point button.

6. Move your mouse over the selected linear features and click the map when the start point is where you want the route measures to start.

7. Click the option for how you want the route measure values to be obtained.

8. Click Make Route.

   The newly created route is now selected.

9. Using any available method, select a simple chain of linear features that form the second half of the loop.

10. Click the Make Route button on the Route Editing toolbar. ▶

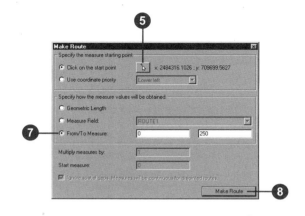

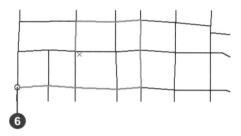

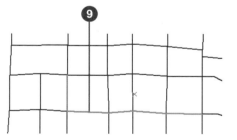

class, the selected set of input linear features will become unselected, and the new route will become selected. This is so that you can set its attributes, such as the route identifier. For more information on editing attributes, see *Editing in ArcMap*.

The process of creating a complex route is similar to that of creating a simple route. The only real difference is that you must build a complex route in pieces. Once the pieces are created, they can be merged together.

The work flow shown here for creating a complex (looping) route is not the only one. With your knowledge of editing in ArcMap, you may choose a work flow that is more appropriate for your organization.

Take note of the fact that in the complex route example shown here, care has been taken to set the measures appropriately for each of the two halves of the route that will eventually be merged together. If this is not possible in your situation, you can still merge the pieces together. Then at a later time, the measure values can be reset. For more information, see 'Remeasuring routes' in this chapter.

11. Click the Start Point button.

12. Move your mouse over the selected linear features and click the map when the start point is where you want the route measures to start.

13. Click how you want the route measure values to be obtained.

14. Click Make Route.

    The newly created route is now selected.

15. Using any available method, select the two routes that will form the loop. ▶

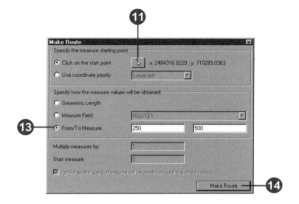

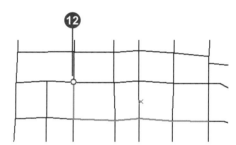

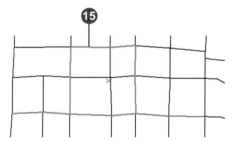

ArcInfo and ArcEditor

Tip

Preserving overlapping segments

The Preserve overlapping segments check box only appears when you are merging two routes. Make sure this box is checked (the default) when you are creating a looping route.

Tip

Setting the selectable layers

Sometimes, when editing, it is easier to edit particular layers by making other layers unselectable. You can set the selectable layers through the Selection menu or in the Selection tab. To learn more, see Using ArcMap.

16. Click the Editor menu and click Merge.

17. Click OK.

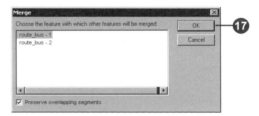

Calibrating routes with points

It is important to have accurate measure values along routes, especially when the measures are used to tie in large amounts of event data.

It is possible to adjust route measures to correspond with known measure locations with a procedure called calibration. *Calibration* adjusts route measures using points. A route can be successfully calibrated with two or more points.

Once you have selected the route that you want to calibrate, you must digitize the points to use for calibration. To digitize the points, you use the Sketch tool. Optionally, you can set the snapping environment. For example, you might want to snap to points that are stored in another feature class. Because one route is calibrated at a time, there is no point-to-route cutoff tolerance specified. All digitized points will be assumed to fall on top of the selected route. ▶

Tip

Undo

If you digitize a point you do not like, click the Undo button ↶ *on the ArcMap Standard toolbar.*

1. Click the Task dropdown arrow and click Calibrate Route Feature.
2. Click the Edit tool, move the mouse pointer over a route feature, then click the feature.
3. Click the Calibrate Route button on the Route Editing toolbar.

   The Calibrate Route dialog box will appear.
4. Click the Sketch tool on the Editor toolbar.
5. Click the map at each location along the route, where you want a calibration point.

   You will see the Calibrate Route point list being populated in the dialog box as you click the points. ▶

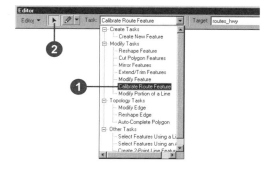

ArcInfo and ArcEditor

Once all the calibration points have been digitized, you must then type the new measure value for each point.

Either whole or partial routes can be calibrated. You can choose to interpolate between the calibration points, extrapolate before the calibration points, extrapolate after the calibration points, or use any combination of these methods.

In order for the measure value on a vertex to be interpolated or extrapolated, a calibration ratio is needed. There are two ways this ratio can be determined. The first method uses the shortest path distance between the input points. The second method uses the existing measure distance between the input points.

When calibrating disjointed routes, you may choose to ignore the distance of the spatial gap between the parts. If you choose to ignore spatial gaps, route measures will be continuous. If you want the spatial gap incorporated in the measures, the gap distance is the straight-line distance between the endpoints of the parts.

Tip

Order is important

Make sure you digitize the calibration points in either route increasing or decreasing order, rather than in some random order.

6. Type the new measure value for each clicked point.

7. Click the calibration options you would like.

8. Click Calibrate Route.

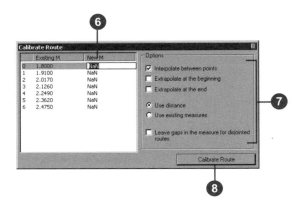

Route measures

Editing existing routes

Whenever a route's geometry is edited in ArcMap, its measure values are edited as well. Because of this, there are three rules that are followed whenever a route's geometry is changed.

First, the measure value on newly added vertices is interpolated when the new vertex falls between two vertices with known measure values.

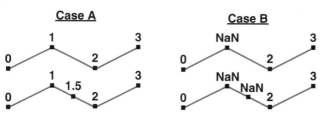

A new vertex will have its measure value interpolated only when it is created between two vertices that have known measure values.

Second, in cases where a route's geometry has been extended, newly added vertices will not have their measure value extrapolated.

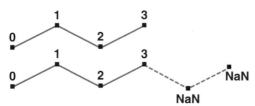

A new vertex will not have its measure value extrapolated when a route is extended.

Finally, certain editing commands, such as Merge, Union, and Intersect, take two or more input geometries and produce an output geometry. In some cases, these commands will encounter situations where the input geometries overlap. Consequently, these commands must choose which of the input feature's measures to use in the output. In such cases, the measure values from the feature that was selected first will be used.

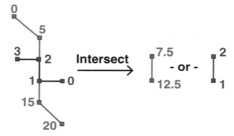

When geometries overlap, some editing commands must choose which of the input feature's measures will be used for the output. In these cases, the measures from the feature that was selected first will be used. In this intersect example, both possible results are shown.

Setting route measures

The following methods can be used to set a route's measure values. It is possible to apply all of these methods to whole or partial routes.

Set As Distance—Set the route's measure values to be the cumulative length from the origin of the geometry. Hence, route measures will increase with the digitized direction of the route.

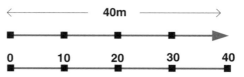

Set measures as the distance from the route's origin.

Set From/To—Set the route's measures using known start and end values. All measure values between the start and end will be interpolated.

In some applications, the ratio between a route's length and its measures is not constant. When the Set From/To method is applied to a route, it is possible to preserve the measure schema that exists. That is, this method can assign measure values based on the original measure value.

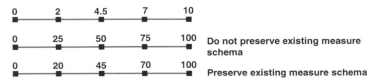

Do not preserve existing measure schema

Preserve existing measure schema

Set the start measure to be 0 and the end measure to be 100. All measure values in between are interpolated.

Sometimes a constant change needs to be applied to a route's measures. This is the case whenever measures need to be rescaled or converted into different units or simply incremented by some value. You can meet these needs by using the next two methods.

Apply Factor—Multiply a route's measures by a factor.

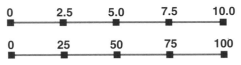

Multiply route measures by a factor of 10.

Offset—Add a value to a route's measures.

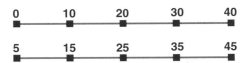

Offset route measures by 5.

Calculate NaN—Interpolate or extrapolate all route measures that are unknown (NaN).

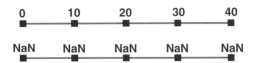

Interpolate or extrapolate unknown measure values.

Drop Measures—Set all route measures to NaN.

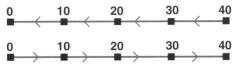

Set all route measures to NaN.

Set Direction As M—There is no requirement that a route's measures increase with the digitized direction. This method will flip a route's geometry to match the direction in which the measures are increasing.

Set a route's digitized direction to match the direction of the measures.

Remeasuring routes

Route measures need to be edited, for example, when more accurate information has been obtained or when the geometry of the route has been altered in some way.

Route measures are edited via an edit sketch. When editing route measures, the edit sketch is simply a shape that represents a copy of the route's geometry. Once you have made the necessary changes to the route measures, you finish the edit sketch. Finishing the sketch writes the sketch geometry to route. ▶

Tip

Edit Sketch Properties
Because route measures are set on an edit sketch, open the Edit Sketch Properties dialog box ⬚ *if you want to see the changes as they happen.*

Tip

Double-clicking to modify a feature
When the Edit tool is selected, you can double-click a feature when you want to modify it. The edit task will automatically change to Modify Feature.

Setting measures as distance

1. Click the Task dropdown arrow and click Modify Feature.

2. Click the Edit tool, move the mouse pointer over the route feature you want to remeasure, then click the feature.

   A copy of the selected route's geometry is written to the edit sketch.

3. Right-click the edit sketch, point to Route Measure Editing, then click Set As Distance.

4. Type the starting measure value and press Enter.

   At this point, the changes to the measures have been applied to the sketch only. To finish the sketch, press F2 or simply unselect the route feature.

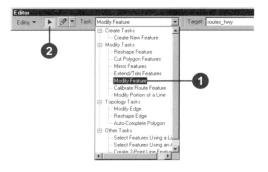

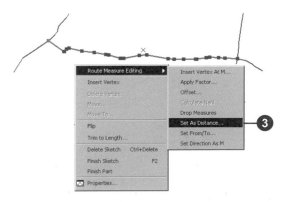

ArcInfo and ArcEditor

Realigning a route is the act of defining a new course for a route. Once a route is realigned, you may need some portions of the route measures to remain unchanged, while other portions need to be updated. Because of this need, it is possible to remeasure whole routes or portions of routes. ▶

Tip

Coordinates or measures out of bounds

If you get the Coordinates or measures out of bounds message when remeasuring a route, it is because the measure values that are being applied to the route do not fit in the m domain.

Tip

Using the Route Measure Editing options multiple times

There are many situations in which you may need to use the Route Measure Editing options more than once to achieve the desired result. For example, you may want the route measures on a new route to be stored in miles. The route feature class, however, has been digitized in feet. An easy solution to this is to first use the Set As Distance option to set the measures in feet. Then the Apply Factor option could be used to convert from feet to miles (the factor would be 0.00018939394).

Setting from/to measures

1. Click the Task dropdown arrow and click Modify Feature.

2. Click the Edit tool, move the mouse pointer over the route feature you want to remeasure, then click the feature.

   A copy of the selected route's geometry is written to the edit sketch.

3. Right-click the edit sketch, point to Route Measure Editing, then click Set From/To.

4. Type the from and to measure values, click whether you want to preserve the existing measure schema, then press Enter.

   At this point, the changes to the measures have been applied to the sketch only. To finish the sketch, press F2 or simply unselect the route feature.

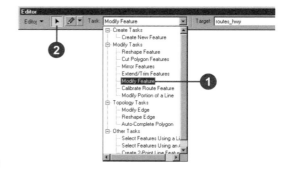

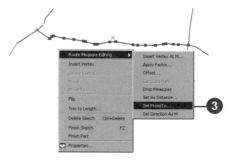

When you are defining a portion of a route to be remeasured, you are actually creating a sketch whose geometry represents just the defined portion. Once the sketch has been created, you use the Route Measure Editing sketch menu—just like you would if you were remeasuring the entire route.

Tip

Context menu

When you are defining a portion of a route, you can right-click the map to display a context menu. The options on this menu allow you to quickly move to any point along the route.

Tip

Map Tip text

When defining a portion of a route to be remeasured, the text of the Map Tip corresponds to the measure value at that point along the selected route.

Tip

Number of decimals

The number of decimals displayed when defining the subportion of a route corresponds to the number of decimals setting on the General tab of the Editing Options dialog box.

Remeasuring a portion of a route

1. Click the Task dropdown arrow and click Modify Portion of a Line.

2. Click the Edit tool, move the mouse pointer over the route feature you want to remeasure, then click the feature.

3. Click the Define Line Portion button.

4. Click a point along the selected route to start defining the portion.

5. Click a second point along the selected route to finish defining the portion.

   An edit sketch is created.

6. Right-click the edit sketch, point to Route Measure Editing, then click the option you want to use to remeasure the portion.

7. After making your changes to the sketch, you need to finish the sketch. To finish the sketch, press F2 or simply unselect the route feature.

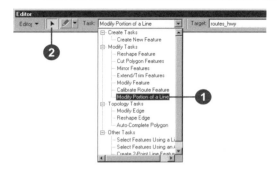

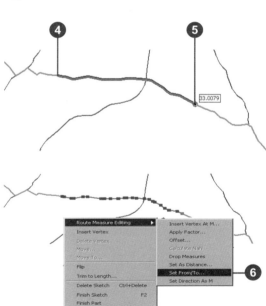

Creating and editing event data 7

An *event table* is just like any other table in ArcGIS Desktop; it is a database component that contains a series of rows and columns. In an event table, each row describes a location along a route, and each column represents a particular attribute about the route location. Event tables are stored in any supported format—for example, INFO™, Microsoft Access, dBASE®, Oracle®, SQL Server™, delimited text files, and databases accessed via OLE DB providers.

In this chapter, you will learn how to create and edit event data and tables. However, before you start creating and editing event data, note that many organizations already maintain large event databases. Quite often, these databases can be accessed and their tables can be used as events without any modification. Any table that contains route identifier and route measure fields—the route location fields—can be used as an event table.

Event tables are generally created in ArcCatalog. Once created, ArcMap makes it easy to view and update the attributes of the events in your database.

Creating and editing event data

Creating event data

In order to be used as an event table, a table must contain route location fields, which are used to find the location of the events along routes.

Event tables can be created in ArcCatalog, where there are tools for creating geodatabase, dBASE, and INFO tables.

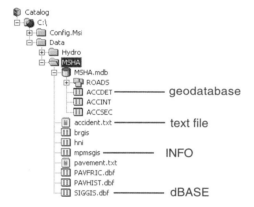

Event data can be stored in any supported table. Shown here are geodatabase, text file, INFO, and dBASE tables.

There are some additional techniques that automate the task of event table creation:

- Creating point events by locating point features along routes
- Creating line events by locating polygon features along routes
- Create line events by locating lines along routes
- Overlaying existing event data to create new line or point events

- Aggregating existing event data using concatenate and dissolve operations
- Transforming route measures from one route reference to another

Overlaying events

In ArcMap, geographic data is represented on a map as a layer. When event data has been added to a map in the form of a layer (see 'Adding route events' in Chapter 5), it can be queried according to feature locations and attributes to solve problems. Further, new spatial relationships can be discovered by asking questions such as Where is...? Where is the closest...? and What intersects...? For more information on how to find answers to these types of questions, see *Using ArcMap*.

Overlaying events is another way to create new event data. This process combines two input event tables to create a single output event table. The new table can be used to analyze event data in ways not possible using traditional spatial analysis techniques.

The new event table can contain either the intersection or the union of the input events. The union of the input events splits all linear events at their intersections and writes them to the new event table. The intersection of the input event tables writes only overlapping events to the output event table.

Line-on-line, line-on-point (same as point-on-line), and even point-on-point event overlays can be performed.

Line-on-line overlay

A *line-on-line overlay* involves the overlay of two line event tables to produce a single line event table.

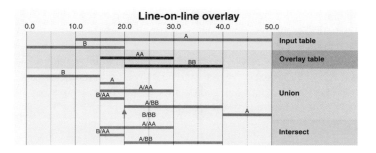

The example below shows the union of a line event table that stores pavement information and another line event table that stores pavement resurfacing dates. The result can be used, for example, to find the characteristics of the oldest paved sections.

RID	FMP	TMP	CRACK
101	23.5	44.2	50
101	44.2	84.7	30
101	84.7	167.4	80
101	167.4	182.8	95
101	182.8	209.5	45

RID	FMP	TMP	RESURF
101	23.5	44.2	2/5/85
101	44.2	84.7	9/3/87
101	84.7	167.4	4/28/61
101	167.4	182.8	1/21/74

RID	FMP	TMP	CRACK	RESURF
101	3.2	21.1	0	2/5/85
101	23.5	44.2	50	9/3/87
101	44.2	84.7	30	9/3/87
101	84.7	95.5	80	9/3/87
101	21.1	23.5	0	9/3/87
101	95.5	167.4	80	4/28/61
101	167.4	182.8	95	4/28/61
101	182.8	190	45	4/28/61

Unioning two event tables can help expose spatial relationships not evident before the overlay. Here, two line event tables are unioned. The output event table contains all of the input events, which have been split where they intersected.

Line-on-point overlay

A *line-on-point overlay* involves the overlay of a line event table and a point event table. The process produces a single point event table.

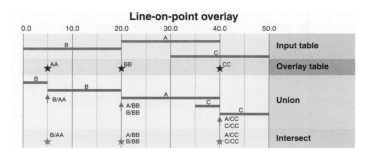

The example below shows the intersection of a point event table containing accident locations and a line event table containing pavement information. The result can be used, for example, to analyze pavement characteristics where accidents occurred.

RID	MILE	INJ	ALC
101	25.9	2	0
101	95.6	1	1
101	172.3	1	0
101	180.3	3	1

RID	FMP	TMP	CRACK
101	23.5	44.2	50
101	44.2	84.7	30
101	84.7	167.4	80
101	167.4	182.8	95
101	182.8	209.5	45

RID	MILE	INJ	ALC	CRACK
101	25.9	2	0	50
101	95.6	1	1	80
101	172.3	1	0	95
101	180.3	3	1	95

Intersecting two event tables can help expose spatial relationships not evident before the overlay. Here, a line and a point event table have been intersected.

Aggregating event data

You aggregate existing event data using *concatenate* and *dissolve* operations. These operations are designed to help maintain the integrity of large event tables.

Both the concatenate and dissolve operations combine event records in tables where there are events on the same route and they have the same value for specified fields. The result is written to a new event table. One difference between the two operations is that concatenate will only combine events in situations where the to-measure of one event matches the from-measure of the next event. Dissolve will combine events when there is measure overlap. Another difference is that the dissolve operation is available for both line and point event tables, while the concatenate operation is available only on line event tables.

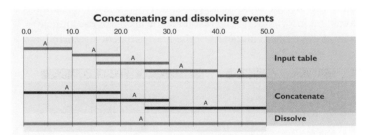

Concatenating and dissolving events combine adjacent records in linear event tables if they are on the same route and have the same values for the dissolve field or fields.

You can use concatenate or dissolve to remove redundant information from an event table. For example, if one linear event in a pavement event table has an attribute—concrete—from 0 to 100, and the following event record has an attribute—concrete—from 100 to 125, the two events will be merged into a single event from 0 to 125. Getting rid of redundant event information makes all subsequent operations on the events more efficient.

RID	FMP	TMP	MATERIAL
1	0	100	concrete
1	100	125	concrete
1	125	175	asphalt
1	175	205	asphalt
1	205	215	concrete

RID	FMP	TMP	MATERIAL
1	0	125	concrete
1	125	205	asphalt
1	205	215	concrete

Concatenating or dissolving events can be used to remove redundant information from event tables.

Another use for concatenate or dissolve is to break up event tables having more than one descriptive attribute into separate tables. For example, if a pavement event table has fields LANES and MATERIAL, the event table can be subdivided into two tables: one having the attribute LANES, and the other having the attribute MATERIAL. To do this, the dissolve or concatenate process would need to be run twice.

RID	FMP	TMP	LANES	MATERIAL
1	0	15	2	concrete
1	15	90	2	asphalt
2	0	125	4	asphalt
2	125	165	2	concrete
2	165	210	4	concrete
3	35	155	2	asphalt

RID	FMP	TMP	LANES
1	0	90	2
2	0	125	4
2	125	165	2
2	165	210	4
3	35	155	2

RID	FMP	TMP	MATERIAL
1	0	15	concrete
1	15	90	asphalt
2	0	125	asphalt
2	125	210	concrete
3	35	155	asphalt

Concatenating or dissolving events can also be used to break up event tables with multiple descriptive attributes.

Transforming event measures

In certain circumstances, it may become necessary to update the measure values in an event table. For example:

- Using an event table to reference multiple route references, each of which has its own unit of measure

- Keeping measures up to date when a route is recalibrated or realigned

Use with multiple route references

In many agencies, event data is collected against multiple route reference systems. For example, a DOT might use both a reference marker system and a milepost system. Some event data, such as accident locations and maintenance activities, is recorded using the reference marker system, while other event data, such as pavement condition or capital improvement projects, is recorded using the milepost system of measurement.

Every year, a DOT manager is required to determine which sections of highway need to be resurfaced. Using a pavement event table, a manager could determine which segments of pavement have fallen into ill repair. The manager does not, however, want to resurface highways with certain types of accident histories without first performing a safety analysis. The reason for this is that speeds may increase on the new pavement, which could increase the accident rate even further.

In order to make a well-informed decision, it will be necessary to combine and analyze the event data that has been collected against the different route references. The pavement scores are based on milepost values, while the accident data is based on reference marker system. To combine the event data, the pavement events must be transformed to the reference marker

system, or the accident events must be transformed to the milepost system.

It is necessary to transform events to analyze events recorded using one route reference with events recorded using another route reference.

In most cases, you will use the ArcToolbox Transform Route Events tool to transform events from one route reference to another. This tool calculates the x,y coordinate location of each event in an input route reference and matches this to the corresponding measure values in a second route reference. The structure of the routes need not be the same. A new event table is written out with the events encoded in a different system of measures.

In cases in which route structure is identical and the difference in measures between two reference systems is constant, a simple mathematical equation can be used to transform event measures. For example, if one route reference has its measures in miles and the other has its measures in feet, then all that needs to be done is to multiply the miles by 5,280 in the field calculator to obtain feet.

Keeping event measures up to date

Measure locations tie an event to a particular location along a route. When the measures of a route are altered, the events will no longer be mapped to the same position along their routes.

In some cases, this is the desired result. For example, if the measures along a stream need calibration to match up to known mileages at gauging stations and the location of fish habitat event data was collected using the gauging stations, then nothing needs to be done to the event data when the route measures are altered.

In other cases, the location of the events when they are mapped must be maintained. For example, if a highway is realigned, the measure of events describing the location of road signs must be updated to maintain their original positions.

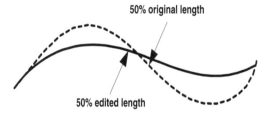

Realigning a route causes measure values to change. Events located on this route will no longer be in the same position.

If changes in route measures are linear along the length of a route, an equation can be applied to the event measures. For example, if a route's measures are multiplied by a factor of 1,000 to convert from kilometers to meters, all event measures can also be multiplied by 1,000.

If changes in route measures are nonlinear, such as what happens during a realignment procedure, then the Transform Route Events tool can be used to recalculate the measures in an event table to maintain the real-world locations.

Locating point features along routes

When you locate point features along routes, you are determining the route and measure information of where your point data intersects your route data.

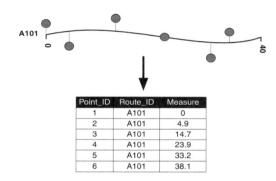

Locating points along routes creates a new point event table containing the route identifier and measure information of where points intersect routes.

Locating point features along routes is useful, for example, when you need to locate:

- Signs along highways
- Wells or gauging stations along river reaches
- Stops along bus routes
- Manholes along city streets
- Valves along pipes

Locating polygon features along routes

Locating polygon features along routes computes the route and measure information at the geometric intersection of polygon data and route data. Once polygon data has been located along routes, the resulting event table can be used, for example, to calculate the length of route that traveled through each polygon.

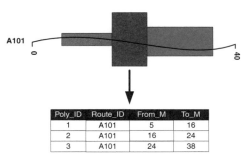

Poly_ID	Route_ID	From_M	To_M
1	A101	5	16
2	A101	16	24
3	A101	24	38

Locating polygon data along routes computes the geometric intersection of the route and polygon data.

Locating polygon features along routes is useful, for example, when you need to locate:

• Soils, spillways, areas of inundation, or hazard zones along river reaches

• Wetlands, hazard zones, or town boundaries along highways

Locating line features along routes

When you locate line features along a route, you are determining the route and measure information where the lines intersect with the route. This intersection is based on a specified cluster tolerance.

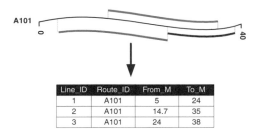

Line_ID	Route_ID	From_M	To_M
1	A101	5	24
2	A101	14.7	35
3	A101	24	38

Locating line features along routes creates a line event table.

Locating line features along routes is useful, for example, when you need to tie them in with your linearly referenced data.

Editing event data

Event tables are only as good as the information they contain. Over time, you will need to modify event data to keep it accurate and up to date. ArcMap lets you edit event data. You can edit any of the attribute values in an event table as well as add and delete event records. You can also use the field calculator to change the attribute value of a field for several events at once.

Creating event tables in ArcCatalog

You can create geodatabase, dBASE, and INFO event tables in ArcCatalog with easy-to-use table designers.

For a table to be considered an event table, it must contain the appropriate route location fields. For point event tables, the required fields are a route identifier field and a measure field. For line events, the required fields are a route identifier field plus both a from- and a to-measure field. All other fields define each point or line event's attribute information. ▶

Tip

Route location fields

The route identifier field can be any numeric or character data type. You should consider creating an attribute index on the route identifier field; it will help improve dynamic segmentation performance. The measure field or fields must be a numeric data type.

See Also

For more information about creating a table in a geodatabase, see Building a Geodatabase.

Creating a table in a geodatabase

1. Right-click the database in the Catalog tree in which you want to create a new table, point to New, then click Table.

2. Type a name for the table. To create an alias for this table, type the alias.

3. Click Next. ▶

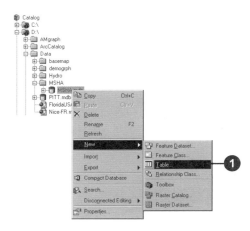

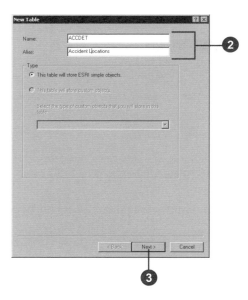

When defining an event table's name and fields, be aware that each database has its own rules defining what names and characters are permitted. Refer to your database's documentation for a list of these rules.

For dBASE tables, the process of defining the attributes is separate from creating the table itself. After creating the table, you need to right-click it in the Catalog tree and click Properties to define the attributes. Because they must contain at least one field, the text field Name1 is added. Add the appropriate fields to the dBASE table, then delete the default field. In a dBASE table, a field name must be 10 characters or less; additional characters will be truncated. ▶

Tip

OBJECTID field in a geodatabase table
The OBJECTID field in a geodatabase table uniquely identifies each object stored in the table. It cannot be deleted.

See Also

For more information about configuration keywords with ArcSDE, see the ArcSDE Configuration and Tuning Guide for <DBMS> PDF file.

If your table does not use ArcSDE, skip to step 5.

4. Click Use configuration keyword and type the keyword if you want to create a table using a custom storage keyword.

5. Click Next.

6. Click the next blank row in the Field Name column and type in a name to add a field to the table.

7. Click in the Data Type column next to the new field's name and click its data type.

8. Click the field next to Alias and type the alias name to create an alias for this field.

9. Click the field next to Allow NULL values and click No to prevent nulls from being stored in this field.

10. Click the field next to Default Value and type the value to associate a default value with this field.

11. Click the field next to Domain and click the domain to associate a domain with this field.

12. Repeat steps 6 through 11 until all the table's fields have been defined.

13. Click Finish.

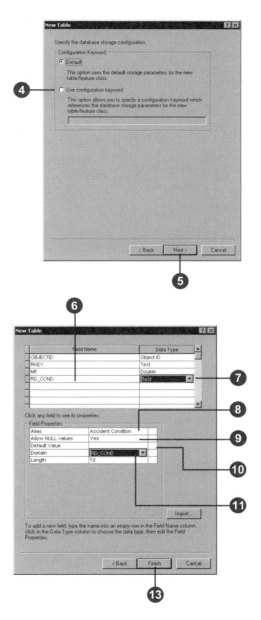

An INFO table's name must be 32 characters or less, and the item names must be 16 characters or less. Items are defined using standard ArcInfo data types. The input width is the maximum number of characters or bytes used to store the item's values. For numeric items, the width must be large enough to accommodate the decimal point and negative sign. The display width is the number of spaces used to display values in ArcInfo Workstation; for decimal values, the display width should be one space greater than the input width to account for the decimal point.

Tip

OID field in a dBASE table

The OID field in a dBASE table is a virtual field that is created by ArcGIS when the table's contents are accessed. It is used to ensure that each object in the table has at least one unique value. It cannot be deleted.

See Also

For more information about creating a dBASE table, see Using ArcCatalog.

Creating a dBASE table

1. Right-click the folder in the Catalog tree in which you want to create the new table, point to New, then click dBASE Table.

   A new dBASE table appears in the folder's contents.

2. Type the name for the table and press Enter.

3. To add a field to the table, right-click the table in the Catalog and click Properties.

4. Click the Fields tab.

5. Click the next blank row in the Field Name column and type in a name.

6. Click in the Data Type column next to the new field's name and click its data type.

7. Click in the Field Properties list and type the properties for the new field.

8. Repeat steps 5 through 7 until all the table's fields have been defined.

9. Click OK.

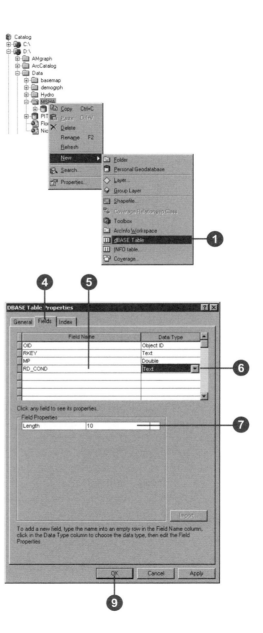

Creating an INFO table

1. Right-click the folder in the Catalog tree in which you want to create the new table, point to New, then click INFO table.

2. Type a name for the new table.

3. Click the data type of the first item in the table.

4. Type the name for the new item.

5. Change the column width, display width, and decimal places as necessary.

6. Click New item to add another item to the table. Then repeat steps 3 through 5 to define the new item's properties.

7. Repeat step 6 until all items have been added to the table.

8. Click OK.

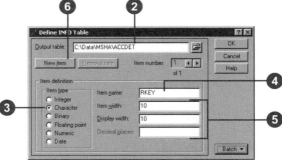

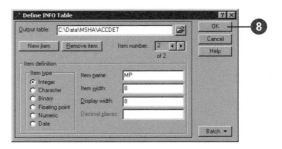

ArcInfo

Overlaying events

The Overlay Route Events tool in ArcToolbox can be used to overlay event tables. Line-on-line, line-on-point, and even point-on-point event overlays can be performed.

To successfully overlay the input event table and overlay event table, both should be based on the same route reference. Otherwise, you may get erroneous results.

The output event table can contain either the intersection or the union of the input events. The union of the input events splits all linear events at their intersections and writes them to the new event table. The intersection of the input event tables writes only overlapping events to the output event table.

If either of the input tables contains point events, the output will always be a point event table. ▶

Tip

Properties that are defined automatically

If you select a layer for either the Input Event Table or Overlay Event Table, the Input Event Table Properties and Overlay Event Table Properties will be set automatically.

Intersecting or unioning overlaying events

1. Click the Show/Hide ArcToolbox button on the Standard toolbar to show ArcToolbox.

2. Expand the Linear Referencing Tools.

3. Double-click the Overlay Route Events tool.

4. Click the Input Event Table Browse button and navigate to the input event table.

   Alternately, click the Input Event Table dropdown arrow and click the input event table or layer.

   NOTE: In ArcCatalog, you will only see a dropdown arrow if an in-memory layer has been created during the session.

5. Click the Route Identifier Field dropdown arrow and click the route identifier field.

6. Click the Event Type dropdown arrow and click POINT or LINE. ▶

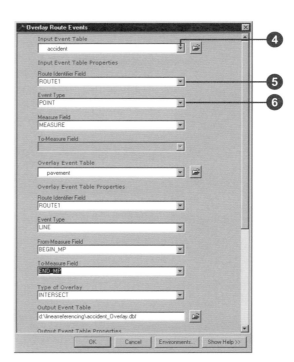

The new event table can be written to the workspace of your choice.

By default, the output event table contains a route identifier field, the measure fields, plus all of the input event attributes. You can choose to not write out the event attributes. In this case, only the respective event layer's OBJECTID field will be written to the output table. This field can be used at a later time to join or relate back to the original event attributes.

When both inputs are line event tables, you can specify whether you want to keep zero length line events in the output table. These are events where the from- and to-measures are equal and can be created by the overlay process.

Tip

Adding the route event table as a layer

You can add a route event table to your map as a layer using either the Make Route Event Layer tool or the Add Route Events dialog box in ArcMap.

7. Click the Measure Field dropdown arrow and click the measure field.

   Depending on whether your output is a point or line event table, you may choose a Measure Field or a From- and To-Measure Field.

8. Click the Overlay Event Table Browse button and navigate to the input event table.

   Alternately, click the Overlay Event Table dropdown arrow and click the input event table or layer.

9. Click the Route Identifier Field dropdown arrow and click the route identifier field.

10. Click the Event Type dropdown arrow and click POINT or LINE.

11. Click the Measure Field dropdown arrow and click the measure field.

12. Click the Type of Overlay dropdown arrow and click either INTERSECT or UNION.

13. Type the Output Event Table filename and path or click the Browse button to specify the output location. ▶

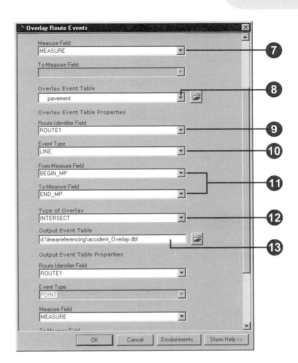

ArcInfo

Tip

Using the ArcMap Route Events Geoprocessing Wizard

You can add the Route Events Geoprocessing Wizard to an ArcMap menu. You can find it in the Tools, Customize dialog box, on the Commands tab, contained in the Linear Referencing category. To learn about customization in ArcMap, see Using ArcMap.

See Also

For information on the optional parameters, click Show Help on the tool's dialog box.

14. Default Output Event Table Properties will be set for you. You may change the suggested field names by clicking any of the active dropdown arrows and selecting an alternative value.

15. Click OK.

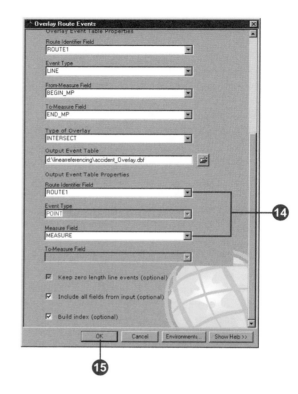

Aggregating events

You can use the Dissolve Route Events tool, in ArcToolbox, to aggregate event data. This tool will combine events that have overlapping measures. Use this tool to remove redundant information from event tables or to break up event tables having more than one descriptive attribute into separate tables. The result will be written to a new event table in the workspace of your choice.

You can dissolve on one or more fields.

Using the ArcMap Route Events Geoprocessing Wizard to dissolve or concatenate events

You can add the Route Events Geoprocessing Wizard to an ArcMap menu. You can find it in the Tools, Customize dialog box, on the Commands tab, contained in the Linear Referencing category. To learn about customization in ArcMap, see Using ArcMap.

Dissolving route events

1. Click the Show/Hide ArcToolbox button on the Standard toolbar to show ArcToolbox.

2. Expand the Linear Referencing Tools.

3. Double-click the Dissolve Route Events tool.

4. Click the Input Event Table Browse button and navigate to the input event table.

   Alternately, click the Input Event Table dropdown arrow and click the input event table.

5. Click the Route Identifier Field dropdown arrow and click the route identifier field.

6. Click the Event Type dropdown arrow and click either POINT or LINE.

7. For point events, click the Measure Field dropdown arrow and click the measure field.

   For line events, click the From-Measure Field dropdown arrow and click the from-measure field. Click the To-Measure Field dropdown arrow and click the to-measure field.

8. Click one or more Dissolve Fields. ▶

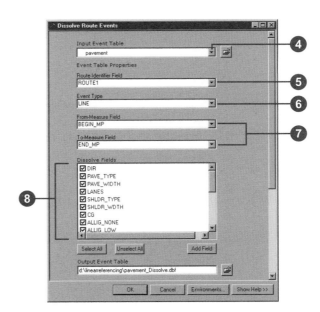

ArcInfo

See Also

For information on the optional parameters, click Show Help on the tool's dialog box.

9. Type the Output Event Table filename and path or click the Browse button to specify the output location.

10. Default Output Event Table Properties will be set for you. You may change the suggested field names by clicking any of the active dropdown arrows and selecting alternative values.

11. Optionally, click Combine adjacent events only.

12. Click OK.

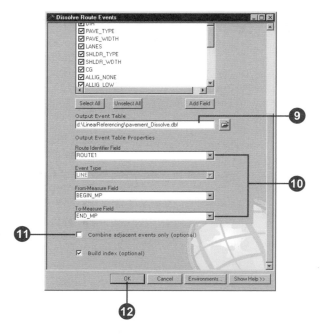

Transforming event measures

There are two ways you can transform event measures. First, in ArcMap, if the required transformation is constant, you can use the field calculator. For example, you can use the field calculator to easily transform event measures between feet and miles.

Second, you can use the Transform Route Events tool to transform one route reference to another. This output will be a new event table.

To be transformed successfully, the input events must be within a specified tolerance of the routes in the target route reference. The default search tolerance is 0. ▶

Tip

Calculating fields outside an edit session
You can calculate field values outside an edit session. You cannot, however, undo your changes.

See Also

For more information on field calculations, see Using ArcMap.

Transforming event measures using the field calculator

1. In ArcMap, click the Editor menu on the Editor toolbar and click Start Editing if you have not already started an edit session.

2. Right-click the table you want to edit in the table of contents and choose Open.

3. Select the records you want to update. If you don't select any, calculations will be applied to all records.

4. Right-click the field heading for which you want to make a calculation and click Calculate Values.

5. Use the Fields list and Functions list to build a calculation expression. You can also edit the expression in the text area below. Lastly, you can type in a value to set the field to.

6. Click OK.

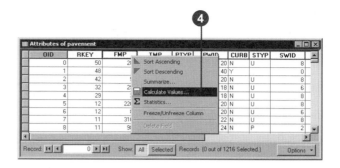

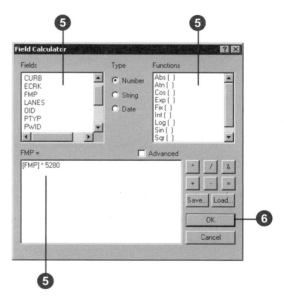

ArcInfo

The output event table contains all of the input event table's attributes, but the route identifier and measure location information are from the target route reference.

Tip

Route structure

When transforming events, the input route structure and target route structure need not be the same.

Tip

Choosing a tolerance

Always use a small tolerance. The larger the tolerance specified, the greater the chance of erroneous results.

Transforming route events

1. Click the Show/Hide ArcToolbox button on the Standard toolbar to show ArcToolbox.

2. Expand the Linear Referencing Tools.

3. Double-click the Transform Route Events tool.

4. Click the Input Event Table Browse button and navigate to the input event table or layer.

   Alternately, click the Input Event Table dropdown arrow and click the input event table or layer.

5. Click the Route Identifier Field dropdown arrow and click the route identifier field.

6. Click the Event Type dropdown arrow and click POINT or LINE.

7. For point events, click the Measure Field dropdown arrow and click the measure field.

   For line events, click the From-Measure Field dropdown arrow and click the from-measure field. Click the To-Measure Field dropdown arrow and click the to-measure field. ▶

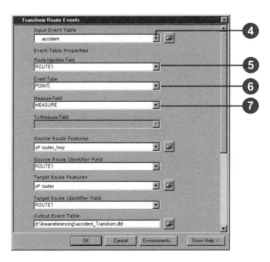

Using the ArcMap Route Events Geoprocessing Wizard to transform event measures

You can add the Route Events Geoprocessing Wizard to an ArcMap menu. You can find it in the Tools, Customize dialog box, on the Commands tab, contained in the Linear Referencing category. To learn about customization in ArcMap, see Using ArcMap.

8. Click the Source Route Features Browse button and navigate to the source route feature class.

   Alternately, click the Source Route Features dropdown arrow and click the source route feature class.

9. Click the Source Route Identifier Field dropdown arrow and click the source route identifier field.

10. Click the Target Route Features dropdown arrow or Browse button to select the target route feature class.

11. Click the Target Route Identifier Field dropdown arrow and click the target route identifier field.

12. Type the Output Event Table filename and path or click the Browse button to specify the output location.

13. Default Output Event Table Properties will be set for you. You may change the suggested field names by clicking any of the active dropdown arrows and selecting an alternative value.

14. Optionally, type a Cluster Tolerance, then click the dropdown arrow and click a unit of measure.

15. Click OK.

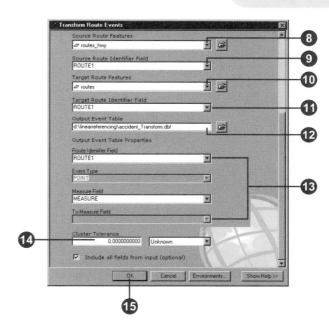

ArcInfo

Locating features along routes

You can locate point, line, or polygon features along routes using the Locate Features Along Routes tool.

When locating point features along routes, the route and measure information of each point feature is computed and written to a point event table. When locating line features along routes, the route and measure information is computed at the intersection of the line and route data and written to a line event table. When locating polygon features along routes, this route and measure information is computed at the geometric intersection of polygon data and route data and written to a line event table.

To be located successfully, the features must be located on or within a specified tolerance of the routes. The default search tolerance is 0. You control the size of the search tolerance by specifying a distance in whichever units you prefer. The search tolerance for points specifies a search radius and for lines it specifies a cluster tolerance. The search tolerance does not apply to polygons. ►

1. Click the Show/Hide ArcToolbox button on the Standard toolbar to show ArcToolbox.

2. Expand the Linear Referencing Tools.

3. Double-click the Locate Features Along Routes tool.

4. Click the Input Features Browse button and navigate to the feature class or layer.

   Alternately, click the dropdown arrow and select the input layer.

5. Click the Input Route Features Browse button and navigate to the feature class or layer.

   Alternately, click the dropdown arrow and select the input layer.

6. Click the Route Identifier Field dropdown arrow and click the route identifier field.

7. If the input is a point feature class, type a search radius.

   If the input is a line feature class, type a cluster tolerance.

   If the input is a polygon feature class, the parameter is disabled.

8. Click the Search Radius dropdown arrow and click a unit of measure. ►

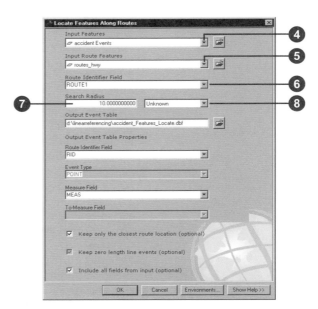

By default, the output event table contains the route identifier and the measure locations; plus all of the attributes from the input feature class.

You can choose to not write out the feature's attributes. In this case only the feature's OBJECTID field will be written to the output table. This field can be used at a later time to join or relate back to the original point attributes.

What is a zero length line event?

A zero length line event occurs when the from- and to-measures are the same. This can happen in locating polygons along routes, for example, when a polygon touches a route but does not overlap it.

For information on the optional parameters, click Show Help on the tool's dialog box.

9. Type the Output Event Table filename and path or click the Browse button to specify the output location.

10. Default Output Event Table Properties will be set for you. You may change the suggested field names by clicking any of the active dropdown arrows and selecting an alternative value.

11. Click OK.

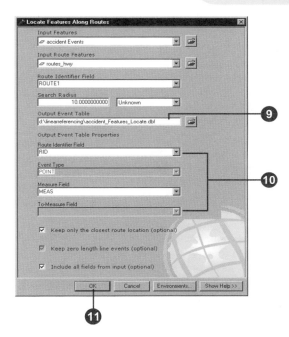

Editing event tables in ArcMap

You can edit event attributes in two ways: using the event's attribute table or using the Attributes dialog box.

As with editing the attributes of any feature, editing event attributes takes place within an *edit session*. You start an edit session by clicking Start Editing from the Editor menu on the Editor toolbar. Once you begin an edit session, you'll notice the Sketch tool 🖉 next to the Options button on the table window, indicating the table can be edited. ▶

Tip
Adding the Editor toolbar
To display the Editor toolbar, click Tools and click Editor Toolbar.

Tip
Saving your edits often
Click the Editor menu and click Save Edits.

Tip
Dynamic segmentation
When displayed as a feature layer, editing an event's route location field will cause the event's location to be dynamically resegmented.

Editing event records using the table window

1. Click the Editor menu and click Start Editing if you have not started an edit session.

2. Open the event table you want to edit.

   You can open either a stand-alone event table or one that has been added to ArcMap as a feature layer. For more information, see 'Adding route events' in Chapter 5.

3. Click the cell containing the attribute value you want to change.

4. Type the value and press Enter.

   The table is updated.

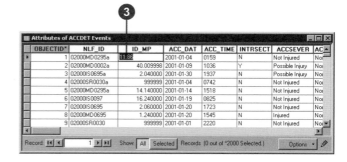

In addition, those fields that you can edit will have a white background color for the field heading.

You make attribute changes by clicking a cell and typing a new value. If you make a mistake, you can easily undo the edit by clicking Undo from the Edit menu.

Editing attributes through the table window allows you to quickly make changes to several records at once. When you're editing the attributes of a specific event, you may find it more convenient to use the Attribute dialog box, which is accessed from the Editor toolbar. To use the Attributes dialog box with events, you must first add your events to ArcMap as a feature layer. For more information, see 'Adding route events' in Chapter 5.

The Attributes dialog box has two sides. The left side lists the features you have selected. Features are listed by their primary display field and are grouped by layer name. ▶

See Also

For more information on table editing techniques, such as copying and pasting records and making simple and advanced field calculations, see Using ArcMap.

Adding new event records using the table window

1. Click the Editor menu and click Start Editing if you have not started an edit session.

2. Open the event table you want to edit.

3. Click the arrow on the right to move to the end of the table.

4. Click a cell in the last record and type in a new value.

   NOTE: If your events table has been added to ArcMap as a feature layer, the new event will appear on the map once valid route location values have been set. For more information, see 'Adding route events' in Chapter 5.

Deleting event records using the table window

1. Click the Editor menu and click Start Editing if you have not started an edit session.

2. Open the event table you want to edit.

3. Select the records you want to delete. Press and hold the Ctrl key while clicking to select more than one record.

4. Press the Delete key on the keyboard.

The right side shows the attribute field names and their values.

When you've completed your edits, you can save them and end the edit session.

Tip

Noneditable fields

If you are editing your events after they have been added to the map as a feature layer, some fields will not be editable. These are the fields that are generated by the dynamic segmentation process: Shape, Loc_Error, and Loc_Angle.

Tip

Events as a feature layer

For events to be edited with the Attributes dialog box, they must be displayed in ArcMap as a feature layer.

Tip

Noneditable tables

Some event tables cannot be edited—for example, delimited text files and tables accessed through an OLE DB connection.

Editing event records using the Attributes dialog box

1. Click the Editor menu and click Start Editing if you have not started an edit session.

2. Click the Edit tool.

3. Select the events whose attributes you want to edit.

4. Click the Attributes button.

5. Click the primary display field of the event feature for which you want to modify an attribute value.

6. Click the value you want to modify.

7. Type a new value and press Enter.

   The attribute is modified for the event feature.

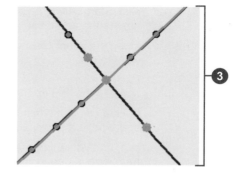

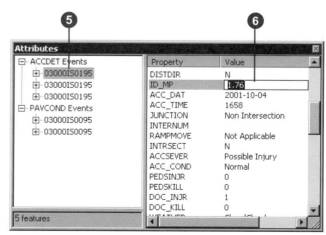

See Also

For more information on editing attributes with the Attributes dialog box, see Editing in ArcMap.

Deleting event records using the Attributes dialog box

1. Click the Editor menu and click Start Editing if you have not started an edit session.

2. Click the Edit tool.

3. Select the event you want to delete.

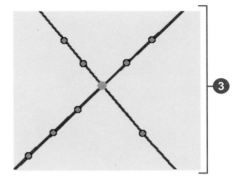

4. Click the Attributes button.

5. Right-click the primary display field of the event feature you want to delete and click Delete.

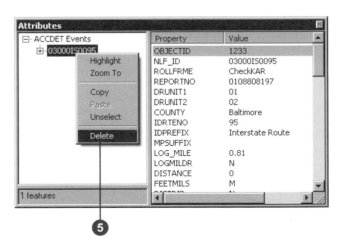

Glossary

alias

An alternative name specified for fields, tables, and feature classes that is more descriptive and user-friendly than the actual name of these items. On computer networks, a single e-mail alias may refer to a group of e-mail addresses. In database management systems, aliases can contain characters, such as spaces, that can't be included in the actual names.

attribute

1. Information about a geographic feature in a GIS, generally stored in a table and linked to the feature by a unique identifier. For example, attributes of a river might include its name, length, and average depth.

2. In raster datasets, information associated with each unique value of raster cells.

3. Cartographic information that specifies how features are displayed and labeled on a map; the cartographic attributes of a river might include line thickness, line length, color, and font.

bookmark

See spatial bookmark.

CAD

A computer-based system for the design, drafting, and display of graphical information. Also known as computer-aided design, such systems are most commonly used to support engineering planning and illustrating activities.

calibration

Comparing the accuracy of an instrument's measurements to a known standard.

Catalog tree

In ArcCatalog, a hierarchical view of folder connections that provide access to GIS data stored on local disks or shared on a network, and allows users to manage connections to databases and GIS servers.

computer-aided design (CAD)

See CAD.

concatenate events

In linear referencing, a command that combines event records in tables containing events on the same route with the same value for specified fields. Only events in situations where the to-measure of one event matches the from-measure of the next event are combined. The concatenate events command is available for line event tables only.

coordinate system

A fixed reference framework superimposed onto the surface of an area to designate the position of a point within it; a reference system consisting of a set of points, lines and/or surfaces, and a set of rules used to define the positions of points in space in either two or three dimensions. The Cartesian coordinate system and the geographic coordinate system used on the earth's surface are common examples of coordinate systems.

coverage

A data model for storing geographic features using ArcInfo software. A coverage stores a set of thematically associated data considered to be a unit. It usually represents a single layer, such as soils, streams, roads, or land use. In a coverage, features are stored as both primary features (points, arcs, polygons) and secondary features (tics, links, annotation). Feature attributes are described and stored independently in feature attribute tables. Coverages cannot be edited in ArcGIS.

database management system (DBMS)

A set of computer programs that organizes the information in a database according to a conceptual schema and provides tools for data input, verification, storage, modification, and retrieval.

DBMS

See database management system (DBMS).

dissolve route events

In linear referencing, a procedure that combines event records in tables where there are events on the same route that have the same value for specified fields. The Dissolve Route Events tool combines events when there is measure overlap and is available for both line and point event tables.

dynamic segmentation

The process of calculating the shapes of point and line route events at run time.

edit session

In ArcMap, the environment in which spatial and attribute editing takes place. After starting an edit session, a user can modify feature locations, geometry, or attributes. Modifications are not saved unless the user explicitly chooses to save them.

Editor toolbar

In ArcMap, a set of tools that allows the creation and modification of features and their attributes.

end hatch definition

In linear referencing, a special type of hatch definition that draws hatch marks only at the low and high measure of a linear feature.

environment settings

Settings that can apply to all tools within the application, all tools within a model or script, or a particular process within a model or script. Environment settings include current workspace, output spatial reference, output spatial grids, cell size, and tile size. They are generally set before running tools.

event

A geographic location stored in tabular rather than spatial form. Event types include address events; route events; x,y events; and temporal events. Address events are features that can be located based on address matching with a street network or other address identifier such as ZIP Codes or lot numbers. Route events are linear, continuous, or point features occurring along a base route system. X,y events are simple coordinate pairs that describe the location of a feature, such as a set of latitude and longitude degrees. Temporal events are used to describe observations through time of particular objects or groups of objects.

event location

See event.

event overlay

In linear referencing, an operation that produces a route event table that is the logical intersection or union of two input route event tables. Event overlay is one way to perform line-on-line, line-on-point, and event point-on-point overlays.

event table

A data source containing location information in tabular format (called events) that is used to create a spatial dataset.

event transform

See transform events.

extrapolation

The inference or calculation of unknown values from values which are currently known; a method or technique of projecting or extending data or inferences beyond known values so as to arrive at conjectural knowledge of unknown data or inferences.

features

A representation of a real-world object on a map. Features can be represented in a GIS as vector data (points, lines, or polygons) or as cells in a raster data format. To be displayed in a GIS, features must have geometry and locational information.

feature class

A collection of geographic features with the same geometry type (such as point, line, or polygon), the same attributes, and the same spatial reference. Feature classes can stand alone within a geodatabase or they can be contained within shapefiles, coverages, or other feature datasets. Feature classes allow homogeneous features to be grouped into a single unit for data storage purposes. For example, highways, primary roads, and secondary roads can be grouped into a line feature class named "roads." In a geodatabase, feature classes can also store annotation and dimensions.

feature dataset

A collection of feature classes stored together that share the same spatial reference; that is, they have the same coordinate system, and their features fall within a common geographic area. Feature classes with different geometry types may be stored in a feature dataset.

field

A column in a table that stores the values for a single attribute.

See also attribute.

GDB

See geodatabase.

geodatabase

An object-oriented data model introduced by ESRI that represents geographic features and attributes as objects and the relationships between objects, but is hosted inside a relational database management system. A geodatabase can store feature classes, feature datasets, nonspatial tables, and relationship classes.

hatch class

In linear referencing, a group or category of hatch definitions.

hatch definition

In linear referencing, a specification for where hatch marks are drawn on a linear feature. Each hatch definition has its own set of properties that include the multiple of the hatch interval at which the hatches in the hatch definition will be placed, the line or marker symbol of the hatches, and whether the hatches will be labeled. The use of multiple hatch definitions allows for the design of complex hatching schemes.

hatch style

In linear referencing, an organized collection of symbols and settings for the hatch definitions that make up a hatch class. Hatch styles are stored in a style file (.style) and created by the user to maintain standards for displaying hatches on multiple maps with multiple data sources.

hatches

In linear referencing, a series of vertical line or marker symbols displayed on top of features at an interval specified in route measure units.

hatching

In linear referencing, a type of labeling that is designed to post and label hatch marks or symbols at a regular interval along measured linear features.

identity

A topological overlay that computes the geometric intersection of two coverages. The output coverage preserves all the features of the first coverage plus those portions of the second (polygon) coverage that overlap the first. For example, a road passing through two counties would be split into two arc features, each with the attributes of the road and the county it passes through.

See also intersect, union.

index

A data structure used to speed the search for records in a database or for spatial features in geographic datasets. In general, unique identifiers stored in a key field point to records or files holding more detailed information.

interpolation

In the context of linear referencing, the calculation of measure values for a route between two known measure values.

intersect

A geometric integration of spatial datasets that preserves features or portions of features that fall within areas common to the input datasets.

See also identity, union.

item

See field.

join

1. Appending the fields of one table to those of another through an attribute or item common to both tables. A join is usually used to attach more attributes to the attribute table of a geographic layer.

2. The process of connecting two or more separate spatial entities. If two line segments are joined, they become one spatial object for further processing.

layer

A set of references to data sources, such as a coverage, geodatabase feature class, raster, and so on, that defines how the data should be displayed on a map. Layers can also define additional properties, such as which features from the data source are included. Layers can also be used as inputs to geoprocessing tools. Layers can be stored in map documents (.mxd) or saved individually as layer files (.lyr).

line

A shape having length and direction but no area, connecting at least two x,y coordinates. Lines represent geographic features too narrow to be displayed as an area at a given scale, such as contours, street centerlines, or streams, or features with no area that form the boundaries of polygons, such as state and county boundary lines.

line event

In linear referencing, a feature that describes a portion of a route using a from- and to-measure value. Examples include pavement quality, salmon spawning grounds, bus fares, pipe widths, and traffic volumes.

linear feature

See line.

linear referencing

A method for storing geographic data by using a relative position along an already existing linear feature; the ability to uniquely identify positions along lines without explicit x,y coordinates. Location is given in terms of a known linear feature and a position, or measure, along it. Linear referencing is an intuitive way to associate multiple sets of attributes to portions of linear features.

See also dynamic segmentation.

line-on-line overlay

In linear referencing, the overlay of two line event tables to produce a single line event table. The new event table can be the logical intersection or union of the input tables.

line-on-point overlay

In linear referencing, the overlay of a line event table and a point event table to produce a single point event table. The new event table can be the logical intersection or union of the input tables.

map

1. A graphic depiction on a flat surface of the physical features of the whole or a part of the earth or other body, or of the heavens, using shapes to represent objects and symbols to describe their nature; at a scale whose representative fraction is less than 1:1. Maps generally use a specified projection and indicate the direction of orientation.

2. The document used in ArcMap to display and work with geographic data. In ArcMap, a map contains one or more layers of geographic data, contained in data frames, and various supporting map elements, such as a scale bar.

map feature

See feature.

map projection

See projection.

map scale

See scale.

MapTip

In ArcGIS, a user-assistance component that displays an onscreen description of a map feature when the mouse is paused over that feature.

measure

See route measure.

measure location fields

In linear referencing, either one or two fields in a table that describe the position of an event along a route.

measure value

See m-value.

m-value

Measure value or vertex attributes. M-values may be added to linear features to perform dynamic segmentation.

NaN

Not a number.

OLE DB provider

Object Linking and Embedding database provider. A tool conforming to the OLE standard for sharing data between applications. Each OLE DB provider communicates with and retrieves data from a different database, but a user can work with the data retrieved by any OLE DB provider in a similar way.

overlay events

See event overlay.

point event

In linear referencing, a feature that occurs at a precise point location along a route; it uses a single measure value. Examples include accident locations along highways, signals along rail lines, bus stops along bus routes, and pumping stations along pipelines.

point-on-line overlay

See line-on-point overlay.

polyline

A two-dimensional feature representing a line containing one or more line segments—that is, any line defined by two or more points. Line features such as boundaries, roads, streams, and streets are usually polylines.

projection

A method by which the curved surface of the earth is portrayed on a flat surface. This generally requires a systematic mathematical transformation of the earth's graticule of lines of longitude and latitude onto a plane. It can be visualized as a transparent globe with a light bulb at its center casting lines of latitude and longitude onto a sheet of paper. Generally, the paper is either flat and placed tangent to the globe (a planar or azimuthal projection), or formed into a cone or cylinder and placed over the globe (cylindrical and conical projections). Every map projection distorts distance, area, shape, direction, or some combination thereof.

raster

A spatial data model that defines space as an array of equally sized cells arranged in rows and columns. Each cell contains an attribute value and location coordinates. Unlike a vector structure, which stores coordinates explicitly, raster coordinates are contained in the ordering of the matrix. Groups of cells that share the same value represent geographic features.

See also vector.

river addressing

In hydrology applications, another name for linear referencing. River addressing allows objects, such as field monitoring stations, which collect information about water quality analysis, toxic release inventories, drinking water supplies, flow, and so on, to be located along a river or stream system.

route

Any linear feature, such as a city, street, highway, river, or pipe, that has a unique identifier and a measurement system stored with the geometry.

Route Editing toolbar

A set of tools that allows you to create and modify routes in ArcMap.

route event

See event.

route event source

In linear referencing, the result of the dynamic segmentation process. A route event source serves an event table as a dynamic feature class. Every row in the table is served as a feature whose shape is calculated when needed. For example, a route event source can act as the basis of a feature layer in ArcMap.

route event table

In linear referencing, a table that stores route locations and their attributes. A route event table, at a minimum, consists of a route identifier field and a measure location field (point events) or fields (line events).

route feature class

See route reference.

route identifier

In linear referencing, a numeric or character value used to identify a route.

route location

In linear referencing, a discrete location along a route (point) or a portion of a route (line). A point route location uses only a single measure value to describe a discrete location along a route. A line route location uses both a from- and to-measure value to describe a portion of a route.

route measure

In linear referencing, a value stored along a linear feature that represents a location relative to the beginning of the feature, or some point along it, rather than as an x,y coordinate. Measures are used to map events such as distance, time, or addresses along linear features.

See also route, dynamic segmentation.

route measure anomalies

In linear referencing, route measure values that do not adhere to the expected behavior. They can often be fixed with ArcMap route editing tools.

route reference

In linear referencing, a collection of routes with a common system of measurement stored in a single feature class (for example, a set of all highways in a county).

scale

The ratio or relationship between a distance or area on a map and on the corresponding distance or area on the ground, commonly expressed as a fraction or ratio. A map scale of 1/100,000 or 1:100,000 means that one unit of measure on the map equals 100,000 of the same unit on the earth.

selected set

A subset of features in a layer or records in a table that is chosen by the user.

shapefile

A vector data storage format for storing the location, shape, and attributes of geographic features. A shapefile is stored in a set of related files and contains one feature class.

sketch

In ArcMap, a shape that represents a feature's geometry. Every existing feature on a map has this alternate form, a sketch, that allows visualization of that feature's composition, with all vertices and segments of the feature visible. When features are edited in ArcMap, the sketch is modified, not the original features. A sketch must be created in order to create a feature. Only line and polygon sketches can be created, since points have neither vertices nor segments.

snapping environment

Settings in the ArcMap Snapping Environment window and Editing Options dialog box that define the conditions in which snapping will occur. These settings include snapping tolerance, snapping properties, and snapping priority.

spatial bookmark

In ArcMap, a shortcut created by the user that identifies a particular geographic location to be saved for later reference.

spatial domain

For a spatial dataset, the defined precision and allowable range for x and y coordinates and for m- and z-values, if present. The spatial domain must be specified by the user when creating a geodatabase feature dataset or standalone feature class.

spatial reference

The coordinate system used to store a spatial dataset. For feature classes and feature datasets within a geodatabase, the spatial reference also includes the spatial domain.

SQL

See Structured Query Language (SQL).

stationing

In the pipeline industry, another name for linear referencing. Stationing allows any point along a pipeline to be uniquely identified.

Structured Query Language (SQL)

A syntax for defining and manipulating data from a relational database. Developed by IBM in the 1970s, SQL has become an industry standard for query languages in most relational database management systems.

symbol

A graphic representation of a geographic feature or feature class on a map. For example, line symbols represent arc features; marker symbols, points; shade symbols, polygons; and text symbols, annotation. Many characteristics define symbols including color, size, angle, and pattern.

table

A set of data elements arranged in rows and columns. Each row represents an individual entity, record, or feature, and each column represents a single field or attribute value. A table has a specified number of columns but can have any number of rows.

topology

The geometric relationships, determined mathematically, between connecting or adjacent features in a geographic dataset. Topology may include information about connectivity, direction, length, adjacency, and polygon definition. Topology makes most types of geographic analysis possible because it allows analysis of spatial relationships between features.

transform events

In linear referencing, an operation that produces a new table by copying and transforming events from one route reference to another. This allows the events to be used with a route reference having different route identifiers and/or measures.

union

A topological overlay of two polygonal spatial datasets that preserve features that fall within the spatial extent of either input dataset; that is, all features from both coverages are retained.

See also intersect and identity.

Universal Transverse Mercator

See UTM.

UTM

Universal Transverse Mercator. A projected coordinate system that divides the world into 60 north and south zones, six degrees wide.

variable

A symbol or quantity that can represent any value or set of values, such as a text string or number. Variables may change depending on how they are used and applied. They are used frequently in mathematics and computing.

vector

A coordinate-based data model that represents geographic features as points, lines, and polygons. Each point feature is represented as a single coordinate pair, while line and polygon features are represented as ordered lists of vertices. Attributes are associated with each feature, as opposed to a raster data model, which associates attributes with grid cells.

See also raster.

vector data model

An abstraction of the real world in which spatial elements are represented in the form of points, lines, and polygons. These are geographically referenced to a coordinate system.

vector model

See vector data model.

vertex

One of a set of ordered x,y coordinate pairs that define a line or polygon feature.

wizard

An interactive user interface that helps a user complete a task one step at a time. It is often implemented as a sequence of dialog boxes that the user can move through, filling in required details. A wizard is usually used for long, difficult, or complex tasks.

workspace

A container for geographic data. A workspace can be a folder that contains shapefiles, an ArcInfo workspace that contains coverages, a geodatabase, or a feature dataset.

zero length line event

In linear referencing, a line event whose from-measure is equal to its to-measure. This can happen, for example, when locating polygons along routes, and a polygon touches a route but does not overlap it.

Index

Precision 59
Projection
  defined 152
Properties
  of hatches 85

Q

Querying
  route data 71, 73

R

Rasters 42
  defined 153
Ratio
  for calibration 114
Realigning
  updating measures 125
Recalibrating
  updating measures 125
Reference scale
  setting 88
Referencing
  linear
    described 41
Relative location
  storing data as 43
Remeasure routes 117
Removing
  redundant info from table 135
River addressing
  defined 153
Road network 43
Rotating labels 100
Route
  complex 107, 111
  data 71
    layer properties 72
  identifier 44

Route (continued)
  locations
    finding 73
    identifying 73
  simple 107, 111
Route data
  adding to a map 19, 33
  calibrating 16
  converting
    coverage to geodatabase 69–70
  creating 14
    measure values are known 51
    measure values are not known 50
  migrating
    to a geodatabase 69–70
  querying 73
Route editing 34
Route Editing toolbar
  adding
    using the Customize dialog box 106
    using the Editor menu 106
  defined 153
Route event source 99
  defined 153
Route event table 102
  automated techniques 122
  concatenating 124
  creating 122
    in a geodatabase 128–129
    in ArcCatalog 128–129
    in dBASE 130
    in INFO 131
  defined 153
  described 46, 121
  dissolving 124
  editing in ArcMap 142–143
  intersecting 123
  measure location 102
  route identifier 102

Route events 45, 99
  adding to a map 101. *See also* Dynamic
    segmentation
  aggregating 135
  defined 153
  described 46, 101
  displaying 101
  dissolving 135–136
  editing 142
  intersecting 122
  overlaying 132, 132–133
  querying 28
  tables 44
  unioning 122
Route Events Geoprocessing Wizard
  aggregating events. *See* Dissolve events
  locating points along routes. *See* Point
    feature
  locating polygons along routes. *See* Polygon
    features
  overlaying events. *See*
    Intersecting; Unioning
  transforming events. *See* Transform events
  using 134, 135, 139
Route feature class
  creating
    in a geodatabase 57
    in an existing feature dataset 60
  defined 153
Route features
  creating 105
  editing 105
Route identifier 102
  creating an index 60, 62
  defined 153
  described 72
  saving 72
  setting 20, 37, 72, 76
  values 74

T

Tables
  defined 155
  noneditable 144
  route events 44
Target annotation
  nonappearing 92
Target feature class 110–111
  setting 34
Text
  on hatches 93
TIN 42
Tolerances
  choosing 138
  of end hatch 77
Tool
  Calibrate Routes 66–68
  Create Routes 64
  Dissolve Route Events 135
  Edit 107
  Locate Features Along Routes 140–141
  Make Route Event Layer 103, 133
  Overlay Route Events 132–133
  Transform Route Events 125, 138
Toolbar
  adding 34
  route editing 106
Topology
  defined 155
  described 47
  with multiple linear referencing methods 47
Transform events. *See also* Route events
  defined 155
Transform Route Events tool 138
Transforming
  event measures 137
    using field calculator 137
    using tool 138
  route events 125

U

Union
  defined 155
Unioning 115
  events. *See* Overlay events
  route events 122, 132
Universal Transverse Mercator (UTM)
  defined 155
Updating
  event measures 125
  measure values 125
UTM (Universal Transverse Mercator)
  defined 155
  described 45

V

Values
  of measure 44, 45
Variable
  defined 155
Vector 42
  defined 155
Vector data model
  defined 155
Vector format
  described 42
Vector model. *See also* Vector data model
  defined 155
  described 43
Vertex
  defined 155

W

Wizard
  defined 155
  Route Events Geoprocessing 134, 135, 139
Workspace
  creating 131
  defined 156

Z

Zero length line event
  defined 156
  described 141